interchange

THIRD EDITION

Jack C. Richards

Intro B

STUDENT'S BOOK

CAMBRIDGE UNIVERSITY PRESS
Cambridge, New York, Melbourne, Madrid, Cape Town, Singapore, São Paulo

Cambridge University Press
40 West 20th Street, New York, NY 10011–4211, USA

www.cambridge.org
Information on this title: www.cambridge.org/9780521601542

First published 2005
2nd printing 2005
Interchange Third Edition Intro Student's Book B has been developed from New Interchange Intro Student's Book B,
first published by Cambridge University Press in 2000.

Printed in Hong Kong, China
Typeface New Century Schoolbook System QuarkXPress®

Art direction, book design, photo research, and layout services: Adventure House, NYC
Audio production: Richard LePage & Associates

ISBN-13   978-0-521-60154-2   paperback
ISBN-10   0-521-60154-1   paperback

To the student

Welcome to *Interchange Third Edition*! This revised edition of *New Interchange* gives you many more opportunities to learn and practice English. I am confident this book will help you improve your English! The course combines topics, functions, and grammar. You will learn the four skills of listening, speaking, reading, and writing, in addition to vocabulary and pronunciation.

Each book has 16 units divided into sections, and each section has its own purpose. The **Snapshot** usually introduces the unit's topic with real-world information. The **Word Power** presents new vocabulary. The **Conversation** is a natural, fun dialog that introduces new grammar. You then see and practice this language in the **Grammar Focus**. The **Pronunciation** exercises help you sound like a native speaker.

In the **Listening** section you hear people speaking in many different contexts. You talk in pairs, in groups, or as a class with the many **Speaking** activities. In the **Interchange activities** you talk even more freely about yourself. These fun activities let you share your own ideas and opinions. Finally, at the end of each unit, you read about and further discuss the unit's topic in the **Reading** section.

Frequent **Progress checks** let you check your own development. In these self-assessment exercises *you* decide what material you need to review.

The **Self-study Audio CD** contains the conversations from the unit for extra listening practice. Your CD also has a section with new, original audio material. You can use this in class, in a lab, or at home with the Self-study exercises at the back of this book.

I think you'll enjoy using this book and hope you become better, more confident learners of English. Good luck!

Jack C. Richards

Author's acknowledgments

A great number of people contributed to the development of *Interchange Third Edition*. Particular thanks are owed to the following:

The **reviewers** using *New Interchange* in the following schools and institutes – their insights and suggestions have helped define the content and format of the third edition: Gino Pumadera, **American School**, Guayaquil, Ecuador; Don Ahn, **APEX**, Seoul, Korea; teachers at **AUA Language Center**, Bangkok, Thailand; Linda Martinez, **Canada College**, Redwood City, California, USA; Rosa Maria Valencia Rodriguez, **CEMARC**, Mexico City, Mexico; Wendel Mendes Dantas, **Central Universitária**, São Paulo, Brazil; Lec Altschuler, **Cheng Kung University**, Tainan, Taiwan; Chun Mao Le, **Cheng Siu Institute of Technology**, Kaohsiung, Taiwan; Selma Alfonso, **Colégio Arquidiocesano**, São Paulo, Brazil; Daniel de Mello Ferraz, **Colégio Camargo Aranha**, São Paulo, Brazil; Paula dos Santos Dames, **Colegio Militar do Rio de Janeiro**, Rio de Janeiro, Brazil; Elizabeth Ortiz, **COPOL-COPEI**, Guayaquil, Ecuador; Alexandre de Oliveira, **First Idiomas**, São Paulo, Brazil; João Franco Júnior, **2B Idiomas**, São Paulo, Brazil; Jo Ellen Kaiser and David Martin, **Fort Lauderdale High School**, Fort Lauderdale, Florida, USA; Azusa Okada, **Hiroshima Shudo University**, Hiroshima, Japan; Sandra Herrera and Rosario Valdiria, **INACAP**, Santiago, Chile; Samara Camilo Tome Costa, **Instituto Brasil-Estados Unidos**, Rio de Janeiro, Brazil; Eric Hamilton, **Instituto Chileno Norteamericano de Cultura**, Santiago, Chile; **ICNA**, Santiago, Chile; Pedro Benites, Carolina Chenett, Elena Montero Hurtado, Patricia Nieto, and Antonio Rios, **Instituto Cultural Peruano Norteamericano (ICPNA)**, Lima, Peru; Vanclei Nascimento, **Instituto Pentágono**, São Paulo, Brazil; Michael T. Thornton, **Interactive College of Technology**, Chamblee, Georgia, USA; Norma Aguilera Celis, **IPN ESCA Santo Tomas**, Mexico City, Mexico; Lewis Barksdale, **Kanazawa Institute of Technology**, Ishikawa, Japan; Clare St. Lawrence, Gill Christie, and Sandra Forrester, **Key Language Services**, Quito, Ecuador; Érik Mesquita, **King's Cross**, São Paulo, Brazil; Robert S. Dobie, **Kojen English Language Schools**, Taipei, Taiwan; Shoko Miyagi, **Madison Area Technical College**, Madison, Wisconsin, USA; Atsuko K. Yamazaki, **Institute of Technologists**, Saitama, Japan; teachers and students at **Institute of Technologists**, Saitama, Japan; Gregory Hadley, **Niigata University of International and Information Studies**, Niigata, Japan; Tony Brewer and Frank Claypool, **Osaka College of Foreign Languages and International Business**, Osaka, Japan; Chris Kerr, **Osaka University of Economics and Law**, Osaka, Japan; Angela Suzete Zumpano, **Personal Language Center**, São Paulo, Brazil; Simon Banha Jr. and Tomas S. Martins, **Phil Young's English School**, Curitiba, Brazil; Mehran Sabet and Bob Diem, **Seigakuin University**, Saitama, Japan; Lily Beam, **Shie Jen University**, Kaohsiung, Taiwan; Ray Sullivan, **Shibuya Kyoiku Gakuen Makuhari Senior and Junior High School**, Chiba, Japan; Robert Gee, **Sugiyama Jogakuen University**, Nagoya, Japan; Arthur Tu, **Taipei YMCA**, Taipei, Taiwan; Hiroko Nishikage, Alan Hawk, Peter Riley, and Peter Anyon, **Taisho University**, Tokyo, Japan; Vera Berk, **Talkative Idiomas**, São Paulo, Brazil; Patrick D. McCoy, **Toyo University**, Saitama, Japan; Kathleen Krokar and Ellen D. Sellergren, **Truman College**, Chicago, Illinois, USA; Gabriela Cortes Sanchez, **UAM-A**, Mexico City, Mexico; Marco A. Mora Piedra, **Universidad de Costa Rica**, San Jose, Costa Rica; Janette Carvalhinho de Oliveira, **Universidade Federal do Espirito Santo**, Vitoria, Brazil; Belem Saint Martin Lozada, **Universidad ISEC**, Colegio del Valle, Mexico City, Mexico; Robert Sanchez Flores, **Universidad Nacional Autonoma de Mexico**, Centro de Lenguas Campus Aragon, Mexico City, Mexico; Bertha Chela de Rodriguez, **Universidad Simòn Bolìvar**, Caracas, Venezuela; Marilyn Johnson, **Washoe High School**, Reno, Nevada, USA; Monika Soens, **Yen Ping Senior High School**, Taipei, Taiwan; Kim Yoon Gyong, **Yonsei University**, Seoul, Korea; and Tania Borges Lobao, **York Language Institute**, Rio de Janeiro, Brazil.

The **editorial** and **production** team:
David Bohlke, Jeff Chen, Yuri Hara, Pam Harris, Paul Heacock, Louisa Hellegers, Lise R. Minovitz, Pat Nelson, Bill Paulk, Danielle Power, Mary Sandre, Tami Savir, Kayo Taguchi, Louisa van Houten, Mary Vaughn, Jennifer Wilkin, and Dorothy Zemach.

And Cambridge University Press **staff** and **advisors**:
Jim Anderson, Angela Andrade, Mary Louise Baez, Carlos Barbisan, Kathleen Corley, Kate Cory-Wright, Elizabeth Fuzikava, Steve Golden, Cecilia Gomez, Heather Gray, Bob Hands, Pauline Ireland, Ken Kingery, Gareth Knight, Nigel McQuitty, João Madureira, Andy Martin, Alejandro Martinez, Carine Mitchell, Mark O'Neil, Tom Price, Dan Schulte, Catherine Shih, Howard Siegelman, Ivan Sorrentino, Alcione Tavares, Koen Van Landeghem, and Ellen Zlotnick.

Plan of Intro Book B

Pronunciation/Listening	Writing/Reading	Interchange Activity
Sentence stress Listening for people's food preferences *Self-study*: Listening to people discuss foods for a party	Writing questions about mealtime habits "Eating for Good Luck": Reading about foods people eat for good luck in the new year	"Food survey": Taking a survey about foods you eat and comparing answers
Pronunciation of *can* and *can't* Listening for people's favorite sports to watch or play; listening to people talk about their abilities *Self-study*: Listening to people discuss sports and activities	Writing questions about sports "Race the U.S.!": Reading about four unusual races in the U.S.	"Hidden talents": Finding out more about your classmates' hidden talents
Reduction of *going to* Listening to people talk about their evening plans *Self-study*: Listening to a conversation about summer events	Writing about weekend plans "What are you going to do on your birthday?": Reading about birthday customs in different places	"Guessing game": Making guesses about a classmate's plans
Sentence intonation Listening to people talk about health problems; listening for medications *Self-study*: Listening to sentences and questions about health	Writing advice for health problems "10 Simple Ways to Improve Your Health": Reading about ways to improve your health	"Helpful advice": Giving advice for some common problems
Compound nouns Listening to people talk about shopping; listening to directions *Self-study*: Listening to people ask for directions	Writing directions "A Walk Up Fifth Avenue": Reading about popular tourist attractions in New York City	"Giving directions": Asking for directions in a neighborhood
Simple past *-ed* endings Listening to people talk about their past summer activities *Self-study*: Listening to conversations about last weekend	Writing about last weekend "Weekend Stories": Reading about three people's weekend experiences	"Past and present": Comparing your classmates' present lives with their childhoods
Negative contractions Listening for places and dates of birth *Self-study*: Listening to an interview with an actress	Writing questions about a famous person's life "Ricky Martin": Reading about a famous singer's life	"Life events": Making a time line of important events in your life
Reduction of *want to* and *have to* Listening to phone conversations; listening to answering machine messages *Self-study*: Listening for mistakes in answering machine messages	Writing messages "Miami, Florida: What's on This Saturday?": Reading about shows and events on a Web page	"Let's make a date!": Making plans with your classmates

9 Broccoli is good for you.

1 WORD POWER Foods

A ▶ Listen and practice.

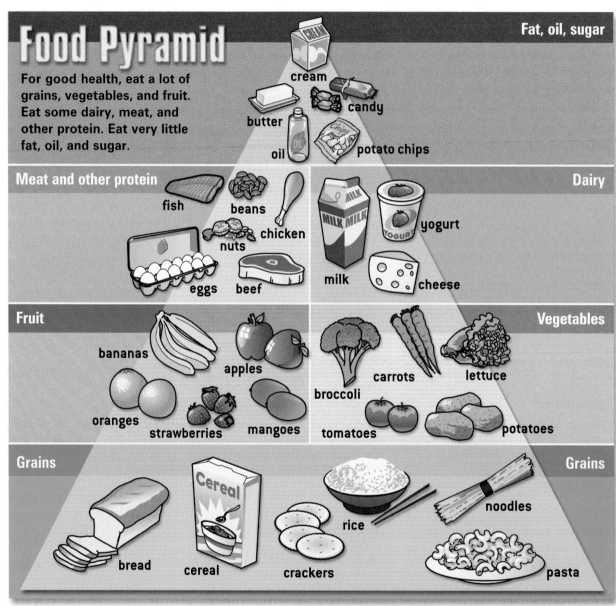

Food Pyramid

For good health, eat a lot of grains, vegetables, and fruit. Eat some dairy, meat, and other protein. Eat very little fat, oil, and sugar.

Fat, oil, sugar

cream
candy
butter
oil
potato chips

Meat and other protein

fish
beans
chicken
nuts
eggs
beef

Dairy

yogurt
milk
cheese

Fruit

bananas
apples
oranges
strawberries
mangoes

Vegetables

carrots
lettuce
broccoli
tomatoes
potatoes

Grains

bread
cereal
crackers
rice
noodles
pasta

Source: Adapted from the U.S. Department of Agriculture Food Guide Pyramid

B What foods do you like? What foods don't you like? Make a list. Then tell a partner.

A: I like rice, potato chips, and carrots.
   I don't like fish, cheese, and bananas.
B: I like . . .

I like	I don't like
rice	fish
potato chips	cheese
carrots	bananas

2 CONVERSATION How about some sandwiches?

A ▶ Listen and practice.

Adam: What do you want for the picnic?
Amanda: Hmm. How about some sandwiches?
Adam: OK. We have some chicken in the
refrigerator, but we don't have any bread.
Amanda: And we don't have any cheese.
Adam: Do we have any drinks?
Amanda: No, we need some.
Adam: All right. Let's get some lemonade.
Amanda: And let's buy some potato salad.
Adam: Sure. Everyone likes potato salad.

B ▶ Listen to the rest of the conversation.
Check (✓) the desserts Adam and Amanda want.

☐ fruit salad   ☐ cake   ☐ pie   ☐ cookies   ☐ ice cream

3 GRAMMAR FOCUS

Some *and* any; *count and noncount nouns* ▶

Do we need **any** eggs?	*Count nouns*	*Specific*
Yes. Let's get **some** (eggs).	**an** egg → egg**s**	I'm eating **an egg.**
No. We **don't** need **any** (eggs).	**a** sandwich → sandwich**es**	Let's get **some bread.**
Do we need **any** bread?	*Noncount nouns*	*General*
Yes. Let's get **some** (bread).	bread	**Eggs are** good for you.
No, we do**n't** need **any** (bread).	lemonade	**Bread is** good for you.

A Complete the conversation with *some* or *any*.

Amanda: The store doesn't have ….*any*…. potato salad.
Adam: Well, we have lots of potatoes. Let's make …………. !
Amanda: OK. Do we have …………. mayonnaise?
Adam: No, we need to buy …………. .
Amanda: We need …………. onions, too.
Adam: Oh, I don't want …………. onions. I hate onions!
Amanda: Then let's get …………. celery.
Adam: No, I don't want …………. celery in my potato salad.
But let's put …………. apples in it.
Amanda: Apples in potato salad? That sounds awful!

B Complete the chart with foods from Exercise 1 on page 58.

Count	Noncount
potatoes	broccoli

C *Group work* Look at your chart from part B. What foods are good for you? What foods are bad for you? Make general statements.

A: Broccoli is good for you, but potatoes are bad for you.
B: Are you sure? I think potatoes are good for you. . . .

 PRONUNCIATION *Sentence stress*

A Listen and practice. Notice the stressed words.

A: What do you need?

B: I need some bread and some fish.

A: Do you need any fruit?

B: Yes. I want some bananas.

B Make a list of foods you need. Then compare with a partner.

5 **SNAPSHOT**

Listen and practice.

What **Do** **You** **Have** **For** **Breakfast?**

The U.S.
- [ ] eggs
- [ ] bacon
- [ ] toast with butter
- [ ] orange juice
- [ ] coffee
- [ ] jam/jelly

Japan
- [ ] fish
- [ ] rice
- [ ] soup
- [ ] pickles
- [ ] green tea

Mexico
- [ ] eggs
- [ ] beans
- [ ] tortillas
- [ ] fresh fruit
- [ ] sweet bread
- [ ] coffee with milk

Source: *www.about.com*

What do you have for breakfast? Check (✓) the foods.
What else do you have for breakfast?

6 *CONVERSATION* Fish for breakfast?

 Listen and practice.

Sarah: Let's have breakfast together on Sunday.
Kumiko: OK. Come to my house. My family always
  has a Japanese-style breakfast on Sundays.
Sarah: Really? What do you have?
Kumiko: We usually have fish, rice, and soup.
Sarah: Fish for breakfast? That's interesting.
Kumiko: Sometimes we have a salad, too.
  And we always have green tea.
Sarah: Well, I never eat fish for breakfast,
  but I like to try new things.

7 *GRAMMAR FOCUS*

Adverbs of frequency

always	
usually	
often	
I **sometimes** eat breakfast.	
hardly ever	
never	
Sometimes I eat breakfast.	

Do you **ever** have fish for breakfast?
  Yes, I **always** do.
  Sometimes I do.
  No, I **never** do.

100%	always
	usually
	often
	sometimes
	hardly ever
0%	never

A Put the adverbs in the correct places. Then practice
with a partner.

  usually
A: What do you have for breakfast? (usually)
            ^
B: Well, I have coffee, cereal, and juice. (often)
A: Do you eat breakfast at work? (ever)
B: I have breakfast at my desk. (sometimes)
A: Do you eat rice for breakfast? (usually)
B: No, I have rice. (hardly ever)

B Unscramble the sentences.

1. I have breakfast on never weekends   *I never have breakfast on weekends.*
2. work I snacks eat at hardly ever   ....
3. eat for pasta dinner sometimes I   ....
4. have I dinner with often family my   ....

C Rewrite the sentences from part B with your own information.
Then compare with a partner.

A: I always have breakfast on weekends.
B: I hardly ever have breakfast on weekends. I usually get up late.

8 LISTENING *Really? Never?*

A  Paul and Megan are talking about food. How often does Megan eat these foods? Listen and check (✓) Often, Sometimes, or Never.

	Often	Sometimes	Never
pasta	✓	☐	☐
hamburgers	☐	☐	☐
fish	☐	☐	☐
eggs	☐	☐	☐
broccoli	☐	☐	☐

B *Group work* Do you ever eat the foods in part A? Tell your classmates.

A: I often eat pasta.
B: Really? I never eat pasta.
C: Well, I . . .

9 MEALTIME HABITS

A Add three questions about mealtime habits to the chart. Then ask a partner the questions and complete the chart.

Mealtime habits	Breakfast	Lunch	Dinner
1. Do you usually eat . . . ?	....	....	....
2. What time do you usually eat . . . ?	....	....	....
3. Do you ever eat meat for . . . ?	....	....	....
4. Do you ever go to a restaurant for . . . ?	....	....	....
5. What do you usually drink for . . . ?	....	....	....
6. What is something you never eat for . . . ?	....	....	....
7.	....	....	....
8.	....	....	....
9.	....	....	....

A: Kiyoshi, do you usually eat breakfast?
B: No, I hardly ever do.

B *Class activity* Tell your classmates about your partner's mealtime habits.

"Kiyoshi hardly ever eats breakfast. But he always eats lunch and dinner. . . ."

 10 INTERCHANGE 9 *Food survey*

Complete a food survey. Go to Interchange 9 at the back of the book.

Eating for Good Luck

On special occasions, do you ever eat any of the foods in these pictures?

On New Year's Day, many people eat special foods for good luck in the new year.

Some Chinese people eat tangerines. Tangerines are round. Round foods end and begin again, like years.

It is a Jewish custom to eat apples with honey for a sweet new year.

Greeks eat *vasilopitta*, bread with a coin inside. Everyone tries to find the coin for luck and money in the new year.

In Spain and some Latin American countries, people eat 12 grapes at midnight on New Year's Eve – one grape for good luck in each month of the new year.

On New Year's Day in Japan, people eat *mochi* – rice cakes – for strength in the new year.

Some Americans from southern states eat black-eyed peas and rice with collard greens. The black-eyed peas are like coins, and the greens are like dollars.

A Read the article. Then correct these sentences.

1. Some Chinese people eat tangerines. Tangerines are ~~sweet~~ *round*, like years.
2. Some Jewish people eat apples with candy for a sweet new year.
3. Greeks eat *vasilopitta*, bread with beans inside.
4. In Europe, people eat 12 grapes for good luck in the new year.
5. The Japanese eat chocolate cake for strength in the new year.
6. Some Americans eat black-eyed peas. Black-eyed peas are like dollars.

B *Group work* Do you eat anything special on New Year's Day for good luck?
Do you do anything special? Tell your classmates.

10 I can't ice-skate very well.

1 SNAPSHOT

▶ Listen and practice.

Sports Seasons in the U.S. and Canada

In the spring, people . . . .
- ☐ play golf
- ☐ play soccer

In the summer, people . . . .
- ☐ play baseball
- ☐ play tennis
- ☐ play volleyball
- ☐ go swimming

In the fall, people . . . .
- ☐ play football
- ☐ go bike riding
- ☐ go hiking

In the winter, people . . . .
- ☐ play hockey
- ☐ play basketball
- ☐ go ice-skating
- ☐ go skiing

Sources: Adapted from *ESPN Information Please Sports Almanac*;
interviews with people between the ages of 18 and 50

What sports are popular in your country? Check (✓) the sports.
Do you like sports? What sports do you play or watch?

2 CONVERSATION *I love sports.*

A ▶ Listen and practice.

Lauren: So, Justin, what do you do in your free time?
 Justin: Well, I love sports.
Lauren: Really? What sports do you like?
 Justin: Hmm. Hockey, baseball, and soccer
 are my favorites.
Lauren: Wow, you're a really good athlete!
 When do you play all these sports?
 Justin: Oh, I don't *play* these sports.
 I just watch them on television!

B *Pair work* What do you do in your free time?
Tell your partner.

64

③ GRAMMAR FOCUS

Simple present Wh-questions ▶

What sports do you play?	I play **hockey** and **baseball**.
Who do you play baseball **with**?	I play with **some friends from work**. We have a team.
Where do you play?	We play **at Hunter Park**.
How often do you practice?	We practice **once or twice a week**.
When do you practice?	We practice **on Sundays**.
What time do you start?	We start **at ten o'clock in the morning**.

A Complete the conversations with the correct Wh-question words. Then practice with a partner.

1. A: I watch sports on television every weekend.
   B: Really? *...What sports...* do you like to watch?
   A: Soccer. It's my favorite!
   B: .... do you usually watch soccer?
   A: On Sunday afternoons.
   B: And .... do you usually watch it? At home?
   A: No, at my friend's house. He has a really big television!

2. A: .... do you go bike riding?
   B: Oh, about once a month.
   A: I love to go bike riding. I go every Sunday.
   B: Really? .... do you go?
   A: Usually at about one o'clock.
   B: Oh, yeah? .... do you usually go with?
   A: My sister. Come with us next time!

B Complete the conversation with questions. Then compare with a partner.

A: *What sports do you like* .... ?
B: I like a lot of sports, but I really love volleyball!
A: .... ?
B: I usually play with my sister and some friends.
A: .... ?
B: We practice on Saturdays.
A: .... ?
B: We start at about noon.
A: .... ?
B: We usually play in our yard, but sometimes we play at the beach.

C *Pair work* Ask your partner five questions about sports. Then tell the class.

A: What sports do you like?
B: I like baseball and soccer.
A: When do you play baseball? . . .

I can't ice-skate very well. • **65**

4 LISTENING *What sports do you like?*

 Listen to the conversations about sports.
Complete the chart.

	Favorite sport	Do they play or watch it?	
		Play	Watch
1. Lisa	*tennis*	✓	☐
2. John	....	☐	☐
3. Sue	....	☐	☐
4. Henry	....	☐	☐

5 CONVERSATION *I can't sing.*

 Listen and practice.

Kayla: Oh, look. There's a talent contest
         on Saturday. Let's enter.
Philip: I can't enter a talent contest.
         What can I do?
Kayla: You can sing really well.
Philip: Oh, thanks. . . . Well, you can, too.
Kayla: Oh, no. I can't sing at all – but I
         can play the piano.
Philip: So maybe we *can* enter the contest.
Kayla: Sure. Why not?
Philip: OK. Let's practice tomorrow!

6 PRONUNCIATION Can *and* can't

A Listen and practice. Notice the pronunciation of **can** and **can't**.

/kən/   /kænt/
I **can** act, but I **can't** sing very well.

B *Pair work* Your partner reads a sentence from
the left or right column. Check (✓) the sentence you hear.

1. ☐ I can sing.   ☐ I can't sing.
2. ☐ I can act.   ☐ I can't act.
3. ☐ I can dance.   ☐ I can't dance.
4. ☐ I can swim.   ☐ I can't swim.

GRAMMAR FOCUS

Can *for ability* ◐

I			you		I		What **can** I do?
You			I		you		You **can** sing.
He	**can**	sing very well.	**Can** he sing?	Yes,	he	**can**.	
She	**can't**	sing at all.	she	No,	she	**can't**.	Who **can** sing?
We			we		we		Philip **can**.
They			they		they		

A Kayla is talking about things she can and can't do.
Complete these sentences. Then compare with a partner.

1. I _can't_ draw.

2. I .... act.

3. I .... sing.

4. I .... fix cars.

5. I .... play tennis.

6. I .... ice-skate very well.

7. I .... play the piano.

8. I .... cook at all.

B *Pair work* Ask and answer questions about the pictures in part A.

A: Can Kayla draw?
B: No, she can't.

C *Group work* Can your classmates do the things in part A? Ask and answer questions.

A: Can you draw, Pedro?
B: No, I can't. How about you, Sachiko?
C: I can't draw. But I can act!

8 LISTENING *I can do that!*

▶ Listen to three people talk about their abilities.
Check (✓) the things they can do well.

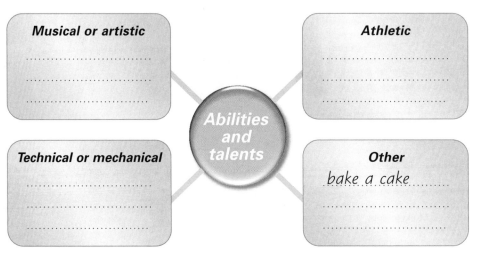

1. Peter	☐	☐	☐	☐	☐	☐	☐	☐
2. Liz	☐	☐	☐	☐	☐	☐	☐	☐
3. Scott	☐	☐	☐	☐	☐	☐	☐	☐

9 WORD POWER

A ▶ Complete the word map with abilities and talents from the list.
Then listen and check.

✓ bake a cake
design a Web page
do gymnastics
fix a car
fix a motorcycle
paint pictures
play chess
play the violin
ride a horse
sing English songs
surf
tell good jokes

Musical or artistic
....
....
....

Athletic
....
....
....

Abilities and talents

Technical or mechanical
....
....
....

Other
bake a cake
....
....

B *Group work* Who can do the things in part A?
Make a list of guesses about your classmates.

A: Who can bake a cake?
B: I bet Sophie can.
C: Who can design a Web page? . . .

bake a cake – Sophie
design a Web page –

C *Class activity* Go around the room and check your guesses.

A: Sophie, can you bake a cake?
B: Yes, I can.

10 INTERCHANGE 10 *Hidden talents*

Learn more about your classmates' hidden talents.
Go to Interchange 10 at the back of the book.

Race the U.S.!

How many different kinds of races can you think of?

Read about four unique American races.

Take eight or ten days to **Race Across America** from Irvine, California, to Savannah, Georgia.

Cross the entire U.S. in this 2,900-mile (4,667 kilometer) bicycle race.

In this race, there are no "time-outs" for sleep. For eight to ten days, racers can sleep only about three hours each day!

Climb the stairs of New York City's Empire State Building in the **Empire State Building Run-Up!**

The climb is 1,050 feet (320 meters) – 86 floors, or 1,575 steps.

Winners can reach the top in just 10 to 11 minutes. Can you?

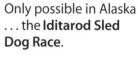

Race on the exciting white waters of the Arkansas River in the **Downriver Race**.

Winners complete the 25.7 miles (41.5 kilometers) in just two hours!

This is the longest downriver race in the U.S. One person. One boat. Take the challenge!

Only possible in Alaska . . . the **Iditarod Sled Dog Race**.

Race from downtown Anchorage to Nome – over 1,150 miles (1,850 kilometers) through cold, wind, and snow.

Winners usually finish the course in 9 to 12 days and receive cash prizes!

A Read the article. Then complete the chart.

	Places	Distances	Winning times
1. Empire State Building Run-Up	....	....	....
2. Race Across America	....	....	....
3. Downriver Race	....	....	....
4. Iditarod Sled Dog Race	....	....	....

B *Group work* Make up a race. What is it called? Where is it? What is the distance? What can you win?

Units 9–10 Progress check

SELF-ASSESSMENT

How well can you do these things? Check (✓) the boxes.

I can	Very well	OK	A little
Talk about foods using *some* and *any* (Ex. 1)	☐	☐	☐
Talk about eating habits using adverbs of frequency (Ex. 2)	☐	☐	☐
Listen to and understand questions about sports (Ex. 3)	☐	☐	☐
Ask and answer simple present Wh-questions (Ex. 4)	☐	☐	☐
Talk about job abilities using *can* (Ex. 5)	☐	☐	☐

1 CLASS PICNIC

Group work Plan a class picnic. Choose two main dishes, two salads, two drinks, and two desserts. Then tell the class.

Main dishes	
Salads	
Drinks	
Desserts	

useful expressions

Do we want any . . . ?
Let's get / make some . . .
I don't want / like . . .

2 SNACK SURVEY

Pair work Does your partner ever eat these snacks?
Ask questions and complete the survey.

	always	usually	sometimes	hardly ever	never
1. popcorn	☐	☐	☐	☐	☐
2. cookies	☐	☐	☐	☐	☐
3. chocolate	☐	☐	☐	☐	☐
4. bananas	☐	☐	☐	☐	☐
5. potato chips	☐	☐	☐	☐	☐
6. apples	☐	☐	☐	☐	☐

A: Do you ever have popcorn as a snack?
B: Yes, I aways have popcorn. OR No, I never have popcorn.

3 LISTENING *What do you play?*

Listen to Jenny ask Ben about sports. Check (✓) Ben's answers.

1. ☐ I play baseball.
   ☐ I play basketball.

2. ☐ Some friends from school.
   ☐ Some friends from work.

3. ☐ At 6:30 P.M.
   ☐ At 6:30 A.M.

4. ☐ Every day.
   ☐ Every week.

5. ☐ On the weekends.
   ☐ In the afternoons.

6. ☐ At the park.
   ☐ In the yard.

4 WHAT DO YOU LIKE?

A Complete the chart with things you love, like, and don't like.

	I love . . .	I like . . .	I don't like . . .
Sports			
Foods			
Clothes			

B *Pair work* Find out what your partner loves, likes, and doesn't like. Then ask more questions with *who*, *where*, *how often*, or *when*.

A: What sports do you love?
B: I love ice-skating.
A: Who do you usually go ice-skating with? . . .

5 JOB ABILITIES

Group work What can these people do well? Make a list.
Use the abilities in the box and your own ideas. Then tell the class.

chef

mechanic

artist

musician

bake
cook
draw
fix a car
fix a motorcycle
paint
play the piano
read music

A: A chef can cook very well.
B: A chef can also bake things, like cakes.
C: Also, a chef can . . .

WHAT'S NEXT?

Look at your Self-assessment again. Do you need to review anything?

11 What are you going to do?

1 MONTHS AND DATES

A ▶ Listen. Practice the months and the dates.

Months	Dates		
January	1st first	11th eleventh	21st twenty-first
February	2nd second	12th twelfth	22nd twenty-second
March	3rd third	13th thirteenth	23rd twenty-third
April	4th fourth	14th fourteenth	24th twenty-fourth
May	5th fifth	15th fifteenth	25th twenty-fifth
June	6th sixth	16th sixteenth	26th twenty-sixth
July	7th seventh	17th seventeenth	27th twenty-seventh
August	8th eighth	18th eighteenth	28th twenty-eighth
September	9th ninth	19th nineteenth	29th twenty-ninth
October	10th tenth	20th twentieth	30th thirtieth
November			31st thirty-first
December			

B *Class activity* Go around the room.
Make a list of your classmates' birthdays.

A: Anna, when's your birthday?
B: July 21st. When's *your* birthday?

> *My classmates' birthdays*
> *Anna – July 21st*

2 CONVERSATION *Happy birthday!*

▶ Listen and practice.

Angie: Are you going to do anything exciting
     this weekend?
Philip: Well, I'm going to celebrate my birthday.
Angie: Fabulous! When is your birthday, exactly?
Philip: It's August ninth – Sunday.
Angie: So what are your plans?
Philip: Well, my friend Kayla is going to
     take me out for dinner.
Angie: Nice! Is she going to order a cake?
Philip: Yeah, and the waiters are probably
     going to sing "Happy Birthday"
     to me. It's so embarrassing.

3 GRAMMAR FOCUS

The future with be going to ▷

Are you **going to do** anything this weekend?	Yes, I am. I**'m going to celebrate** my birthday. No, I'm not. I**'m going to stay home**.
Is Kayla **going to have** a party for you?	Yes, she is. She**'s going to invite** all my friends. No, she isn't. She**'s going to take** me **out** for dinner.
Are the waiters **going to sing** to you?	Yes, they are. They**'re going to sing** "Happy Birthday." No, they aren't. But they**'re going to give** me a cake.

A What are these people going to do this weekend?
Write sentences. Then compare with a partner.

1. They're going to go dancing.
2. She's going to read.

B *Pair work* Is your partner going to do the things in part A
this weekend? Ask and answer questions.

A: Are you going to go dancing this weekend?
B: Yes, I am. I'm going to go to a new dance club downtown.
A: Are you going to go with a friend? . . .

4 INTERCHANGE 11 Guessing game

Make guesses about your classmates' plans. Go to Interchange 11.

What are you going to do? • **73**

5 PRONUNCIATION Reduction of going to

A ▶ Listen and practice. Notice the reduction of **going to** to /gənə/.

A: Are you **going to** have a party?
B: No, I'm **going to** go out with a friend.

A: Are you **going to** go to a restaurant?
B: Yes. We're **going to** go to Nick's Café.

B *Pair work* Ask your partner about his or her weekend plans. Try to reduce **going to**.

6 LISTENING Evening plans

A It's 5:30 P.M. What are these people's evening plans? Write your guesses in the chart.

B ▶ Listen to the interviewer ask these people about their plans. What are they really going to do? Complete the chart.

Michelle   Kevin   Robert   Jane

Your guess	What they're really going to do
Michelle *is going to go to the gym* .	Michelle ....
Kevin	Kevin ....
Robert	Robert ....
Jane	Jane ....

7 SNAPSHOT

 Listen and practice.

Source: *The Concise Columbia Encyclopedia*

Do you celebrate any of these holidays? How do you celebrate them?
What are some holidays in your country? What's your favorite holiday?

CONVERSATION *Have a good Valentine's Day.*

 Listen and practice.

Mona: So, Tyler, are you going to do anything special for Valentine's Day?
Tyler: Yeah, I'm going to take my girlfriend out for dinner.
Mona: Oh, really? Where are you going to go?
Tyler: Laguna's. It's her favorite restaurant.
Mona: Oh, she's going to like that!
Tyler: How about you? What are you going to do?
Mona: Well, I'm not going to go to a restaurant, but I am going to go to a dance.
Tyler: Sounds like fun. Well, have a good Valentine's Day.
Mona: Thanks. You, too.

9 **GRAMMAR FOCUS**

What are you going to do for Valentine's Day?	**How are you going to get** there?
I**'m going to go** to a dance.	We**'re going to drive.**
I**'m not going to go** to a restaurant.	We**'re not going to take** a bus.
Where are you going to go?	**Who's going to be** there?
We**'re going to go** to Laguna's.	My friends **are going to be** there.
We**'re not going to stay** home.	My sister **isn't going to be** there.

A Complete this conversation with the correct form of *be going to.*
Then practice with a partner.

A: What ..*are*.. you ...*going to do*...... (do) for Halloween?
B: I don't know. I .... (not do) anything special.
A: Well, Pat and I .... (have) a party. Can you come?
B: Sure! Where .... you .... (have) the party?
A: It .... (be) at Pat's house.
B: What time .... the party .... (start)?
A: At 6:00. And it .... (end) around midnight.
B: Who .... you .... (invite)?
A: We .... (ask) all our good friends.

B *Group work* Ask your classmates about their plans.
Use the time expressions in the box.

A: What are you going to do tonight?
B: I'm going to go to a party.
C: Oh, really? Who's going to be there?
B: Well, Lara and Rosa are going to come.
But Jeff isn't going to be there. . . .

time expressions	
tonight	next week
tomorrow	next month
tomorrow night	next summer

10 WORD POWER *Special occasions*

A ▶ Listen and practice. Then check (✓) the things you do for each special occasion.

	Mother's Day	Father's Day	Graduation	Wedding	Anniversary
send cards	☐	☐	☐	☐	☐
give presents	☐	☐	☐	☐	☐
take pictures	☐	☐	☐	☐	☐
sing songs	☐	☐	☐	☐	☐
dance	☐	☐	☐	☐	☐
eat cake	☐	☐	☐	☐	☐
have a party	☐	☐	☐	☐	☐
have a picnic	☐	☐	☐	☐	☐
eat special food	☐	☐	☐	☐	☐
wear special clothes	☐	☐	☐	☐	☐

B *Group work* What special occasions are you going to celebrate this year? When are they? How are you going to celebrate them? Ask your classmates.

A: What special occasions are you going to celebrate this year?
B: I'm going to go to my sister's wedding.
C: Really? When is she going to get married?

11 HOLIDAYS AND FESTIVALS

A *Pair work* Choose any holiday or festival you like. Then ask and answer these questions.

What is the holiday or festival?
When is it?
What are you going to do?
Where are you going to go?
Who's going to be there?
When are you going to go?
How are you going to get there?

A: What is the holiday or festival?
B: It's Cinco de Mayo.
A: When is it?
B: It's on May fifth.
A: What are you going to do?
B: I'm going to go to a parade. . . .

B *Class activity* Tell the class about your partner's plans.

Setsubun in Japan

Cinco de Mayo in Mexico

Eid in Pakistan

12 READING ▶

What are you going to do
on your
birthday?

> **Scan the article. How old is each person going to be?**

Elena Buenaventura
Madrid
"My twenty-first birthday is on Saturday, and I'm going to go out with some friends. To wish me a happy birthday, they're going to pull on my ear 21 times – once for each year. It's an old custom. Some people pull on the ear just once, but my friends are very traditional!"

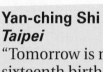

Yan-ching Shi
Taipei
"Tomorrow is my sixteenth birthday. It's a special birthday, so we're going to have a family ceremony. I'm probably going to get some money in 'lucky' envelopes from my relatives. My mother is going to cook noodles – noodles are for a long life."

Mr. and Mrs. Aoki
Kyoto
"My husband is going to be 60 tomorrow. In Japan, the sixtieth birthday is called *kanreki* – it's the beginning of a new life. The color red represents a new life, so children often give something red as a present. What are our children going to give him? A red hat and vest!"

Philippe Joly
Paris
"I'm going to be 30 next week, so I'm going to invite three very good friends out to dinner. In France, when you have a birthday, you often invite people out. In some countries, I know it's the opposite – people take you out."

A Read the article. Then correct these sentences.

1. To celebrate her birthday, Elena is going to pull on her friends' ears.
2. Yan-Ching is going to cook some noodles on her birthday.
3. On his birthday, Mr. Aoki is going to buy something red.
4. Philippe's friends are going to take him out to dinner on his birthday.

B *Group work* How do people usually celebrate birthdays in your country?
Do you have plans for your next birthday? How about the birthday of a friend
or family member? What are you going to do? Tell your classmates.

12 What's the matter?

WORD POWER *Parts of the body*

A ▶ Listen and practice.

head
eye
ear
nose

mouth
tooth/teeth
chin

wrist
arm
elbow

back
shoulder
chest
stomach

throat
neck

thumb
hand
finger(s)

leg
knee
ankle

foot/feet
toe(s)

B *Pair work* Close your books. Tell your partner to point to the parts of the body.

A: Point to your neck.
B: This is my neck.
   Point to your feet.
A: These are my feet.

CONVERSATION *I feel homesick.*

 Listen and practice.

Brian: Hey, Kenichi. How are you?
Kenichi: Oh, I'm not so good, actually.
Brian: Why? What's the matter?
Kenichi: Well, I have a headache. And a backache.
Brian: Maybe you have the flu.
Kenichi: No, I think I just feel a little
homesick for Japan.
Brian: That's too bad. . . . But maybe I can help.
Let's have lunch at that new Japanese
restaurant.
Kenichi: That's a great idea. Thanks, Brian.
I feel better already!

③ GRAMMAR FOCUS

Have + *noun;* feel + *adjective*

What's the matter? What's wrong?	How are you? How do you feel?	Negative adjectives	Positive adjectives
I have a headache.	**I feel homesick.**	sick	fine
I have a backache.	**I feel better.**	awful	great
I have the flu.	**I don't feel well.**	terrible	terrific
		miserable	fantastic

A Listen and practice. *"He has a backache."*

  a backache   an earache   a headache   a stomachache   a toothache

   a cold   a cough   a fever   the flu   sore eyes   a sore throat

B *Pair work* Act out a health problem. Your partner guesses the problem.

A: What's wrong? Do you have a headache?
B: No, I don't.
A: Do you have an earache?
B: Yes, that's right!

C *Class activity* Go around the class. Find out how your classmates feel today. Respond with an expression from the box.

A: How do you feel today, Jun?
B: I feel fine, thanks. What about you, Leo?
A: I feel terrible. I have a stomachache.
B: I'm sorry to hear that.

expressions
That's good.
I'm glad to hear that.
That's too bad.
I'm sorry to hear that.

 4 **LISTENING** *I have a headache.*

A Listen to the conversations. Where do these people hurt? Write down the parts of the body.

1. Ben
   head, throat
2. Alison
3. Jeffrey
4. Marta

B *Pair work* Ask and answer questions about the people in part A.

A: What's the matter with Ben?
B: He has a headache and a sore throat.

5 **SNAPSHOT**

Listen and practice.

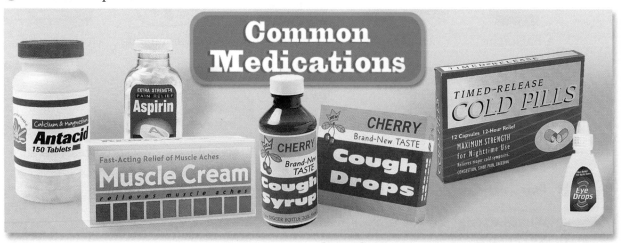

Common Medications

Sources: Based on information from *Almanac of the American People* and interviews with people between the ages of 25 and 50

What medications do you have at home?
What are these medications for?

6 *CONVERSATION* Don't work too hard.

 Listen and practice.

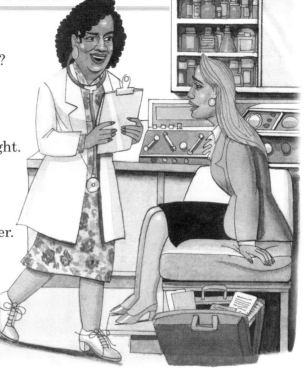

Dr. Young: Hello, Ms. West. How are you today?
Ms. West: Not so good.
Dr. Young: So, what's wrong, exactly?
Ms. West: I'm exhausted!
Dr. Young: Hmm. Why are you so tired?
Ms. West: I don't know. I just can't sleep at night.
Dr. Young: OK. Let's take a look at you.

A few minutes later

Dr. Young: I'm going to give you some pills.
Take one pill every night after dinner.
Ms. West: OK.
Dr. Young: And don't drink coffee, tea, or soda.
Ms. West: Anything else?
Dr. Young: Yes. Don't work too hard.
Ms. West: All right. Thanks,
Dr. Young.

7 *LISTENING* Let's take a look.

 Listen to Dr. Young talk to four other patients. What does she give them? Check (✓) the correct medications.

	Antacid	Aspirin	Cold pills	Eye drops	Muscle cream
1. Ben	☐	☐	☐	☐	☐
2. Alison	☐	☐	☐	☐	☐
3. Jeffrey	☐	☐	☐	☐	☐
4. Marta	☐	☐	☐	☐	☐

8 *PRONUNCIATION* Sentence intonation

A Listen and practice. Notice the intonation in these sentences.

Take some aspirin.   Don't drink coffee.

Go to bed.   Don't work too hard.

Use some muscle cream.   Don't exercise this week.

B *Pair work* Practice the conversation in Exercise 6 again.
Pay attention to the sentence intonation.

9 GRAMMAR FOCUS

Imperatives ▷

Take a pill every four hours.
Rest in bed.
Drink lots of juice.

Don't work too hard.
Don't stay up late.
Don't drink soda.

A Complete these sentences. Use the correct forms of the words in the box.

✓ call	see	not go	not drink
listen	take	✓ not worry	not eat

1. *....Call....* a dentist.
2. *..Don't worry..* too much.
3. .... two aspirin.
4. .... to school.

5. .... to relaxing music.
6. .... a doctor.
7. .... coffee.
8. .... any candy.

B Write two pieces of advice for each problem. Use the sentences from part A or your own ideas.

I have a toothache.

I have a headache.

I have the flu.

I can't sleep at night.

1. *Call a dentist.*
....

2. ....
....

3. ....
....

4. ....
....

C *Pair work* Act out the problems from part B. Your partner gives advice.

A: I feel miserable!
B: What's the matter?
A: I have a terrible toothache!
B: I have an idea. Call a dentist. . . .

10 INTERCHANGE 12 *Helpful advice*

Give advice for some common problems. Go to Interchange 12.

82 • Unit 12

10 Simple Ways
to Improve Your Health

Can you think of some ways to improve your health? Don't look at the article.

Believe it or not, you can greatly improve your health in ten simple ways.

1 Eat breakfast. Breakfast gives you energy for the morning.

2 Go for a walk. Walking is good exercise, and exercise is necessary for good health.

3 Floss your teeth. Don't just brush them. Flossing keeps your gums healthy.

4 Drink eight cups of water every day. Water helps your body in many ways.

5 Stretch for five minutes. Stretching is important for your muscles.

6 Wear a seat belt. Every year, seat belts save thousands of lives.

7 Do something to challenge your brain. For example, do a crossword puzzle or read a new book.

8 Protect your skin. Use lots of moisturizer and sunscreen.

9 Get enough calcium. Your bones need it. Dairy foods, like yogurt, milk, and cheese, have calcium.

10 Take a "time-out" – a break of about 20 minutes. Do something different. For example, get up and walk. Or sit down and listen to music.

Source: *Cooking Light* ® Magazine

A Read the article. Then complete the sentences.

1. To get exercise, _go for a walk_ .
2. To help your bones, .
3. To help your muscles, .
4. To keep your gums healthy, .
5. To have energy for the morning, .
6. To challenge your brain, .

B *Group work* What things in the article do you do regularly?
What else do you do for your health? Tell your classmates.

Units 11–12 Progress check

SELF-ASSESSMENT

How well can you do these things? Check (✓) the boxes.

I can	Very well	OK	A little
Ask and answer yes/no questions about holidays with *be going to* (Ex. 1)	☐	☐	☐
Ask and answer Wh-questions about future plans with *be going to* (Ex. 2)	☐	☐	☐
Use future time expressions (Ex. 2)	☐	☐	☐
Listen to and understand conversations about problems (Ex. 3)	☐	☐	☐
Talk about problems using *have* + noun and *feel* + adjective (Ex. 4)	☐	☐	☐
Give advice using imperatives (Ex. 4)	☐	☐	☐

1 HOLIDAY SURVEY

A Complete the questions with names of different holidays.

Are you going to . . . ?	Name
dance on	....
give presents on	....
have a party on	....
send cards on	....
take photos on	....

B *Class activity* Are your classmates going to do the things in part A? Go around the class and find this information. Try to write a different name on each line.

2 PLANS, PLANS, PLANS

Complete these questions with different time expressions.
Then ask a partner the questions.

1. How are you going to get home *tonight* .... ?
2. What time are you going to go to bed .... ?
3. Who's going to be here .... ?
4. Where are you going to go .... ?
5. What are you going to do .... ?
6. Who are you going to eat dinner with .... ?

3 LISTENING What's the matter?

Listen to six conversations. Number the pictures from 1 to 6.

.... This person needs some ketchup.

.... This person has a backache.

.... This person can't dance very well.

..1.. This person feels sad.

.... This person is going to take a test tomorrow.

.... This person has the flu.

4 THAT'S GREAT ADVICE!

A Write a problem on a piece of paper. Then write advice for the problem on a different piece of paper.

> I'm homesick.

> Call your family.

B *Class activity* Put the papers with problems and the papers with advice in two different boxes. Then take a new paper from each box. Go around the class and find the right advice for your problem.

A: I feel terrible.
B: What's the matter?
A: I'm homesick.
B: Maybe I can help. See a dentist.
A: That's terrible advice!

A: I feel awful.
C: Why? What's wrong?
A: I'm homesick.
C: I know! Call your family.
A: That's great advice. Thanks!

WHAT'S NEXT?

Look at your Self-assessment again. Do you need to review anything?

13 You can't miss it.

1 WORD POWER Places and things

A ▶ Where can you get these things? Match the things with the places. Then listen and practice. *"You can buy aspirin at a drugstore."*

1. aspirin ...b...
2. bread ....
3. a dictionary ....
4. gasoline ....
5. a sandwich ....
6. stamps ....
7. a sweatshirt ....
8. traveler's checks ....

a. a bank

b. a drugstore

c. a post office

d. a gas station

e. a restaurant

f. a bookstore

g. a department store

h. a supermarket

B *Pair work* What else can you get or do in the places in part A? Make a list.

A: You can get money at a bank.
B: You can also . . .

LISTENING *I need a new swimsuit.*

A Listen to the Anderson family's conversations. What do they need? Where are they going to buy them? Complete the chart.

	What	**Where**
1. Jean	*a swimsuit*	
2. Mom		*the supermarket*
3. Dad		
4. Mike		

B *Pair work* What do you need? Where are you going to buy it? Tell your partner.

"I need a dictionary, so I'm going to go to a bookstore. . . ."

CONVERSATION *It's across from the park.*

 Listen and practice.

Man: Excuse me. Can you help me? Is there a public rest room around here?

Woman: A public rest room? Hmm. I'm sorry. I don't think so.

Man: Oh, no. My son needs a rest room.

Woman: Well, there's a rest room in the department store on Main Street.

Man: Where on Main Street?

Woman: It's on the corner of Main and First Avenue.

Man: On the corner of Main and First?

Woman: Yes, it's across from the park. You can't miss it.

Man: Thanks a lot.

PRONUNCIATION *Compound nouns*

Listen and practice. Notice the stress in these compound nouns.

post office   gas station   rest room   coffee shop

drugstore   supermarket   bookstore   department store

5 GRAMMAR FOCUS

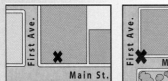

| on | on the corner of | across from | next to | between |

The department store is **on** Main Street.
It's **on the corner of** Main and First.
It's **across from** the park.

It's **next to** the bank.
The bank is **between** the department store **and** the restaurant.

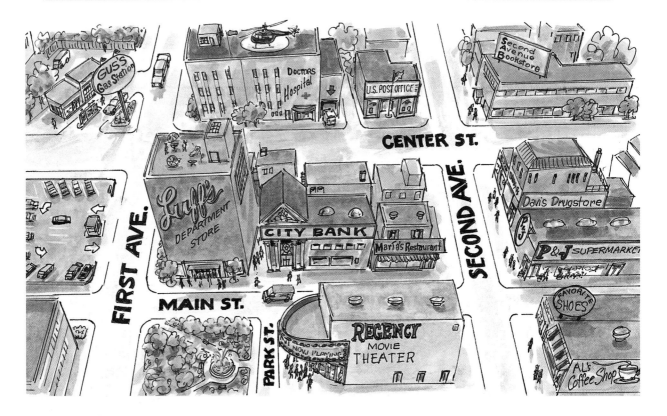

A Look at the map and complete the sentences. Then compare with a partner.

1. The coffee shop is ....*on*........ Second Avenue. It's .... the shoe store.
2. The movie theater is .... Park and Main. It's .... the park.
3. The gas station is .... the parking lot. It's .... First and Center.
4. The drugstore is .... Center and Second. It's .... the supermarket.
5. The bank is .... the restaurant and the department store.
   It's .... Main Street.

B *Pair work* Where are these places on the map? Ask and answer questions.

the park   the post office   the bookstore   the hospital   the shoe store

A: Where is the park?
B: It's between Park and First, across from the department store.

6 LISTENING *Where is it?*

Look at the map in Exercise 5. Listen to four conversations. Where are the people going?

1. *the bank* .... 　2. .... 　3. .... 　4. ....

7 SNAPSHOT

Listen and practice.

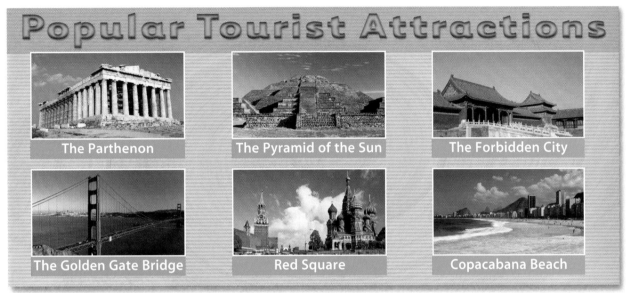

Popular Tourist Attractions

| The Parthenon | The Pyramid of the Sun | The Forbidden City |
| The Golden Gate Bridge | Red Square | Copacabana Beach |

Sources: *www.infoplease.com*; *www.fodors.com*

Where are these places? What do you know about them?
What tourist attractions in your country are popular? Why?

8 CONVERSATION *Is it far from here?*

Listen and practice.

Tourist: Excuse me, ma'am. Can you help me? How do I get to St. Patrick's Cathedral?

Woman: Just walk up Fifth Avenue to 50th Street. St. Patrick's is on the right.

Tourist: Is it near Rockefeller Center?

Woman: Yes, it's right across from Rockefeller Center.

Tourist: Thank you. And where is the Empire State Building? Is it far from here?

Woman: It's right behind you. Just turn around and look up!

9 GRAMMAR FOCUS

Directions ▶

How do I get to Rockefeller Center?	**How can I get to** Bryant Park?
Walk up/Go up Fifth Avenue.	**Walk down/Go down** Fifth Avenue.
Turn left on 49th Street.	**Turn right on** 42nd Street.
It's **on the right**.	It's **on the left**.

Pair work Imagine you are tourists at Grand Central Terminal.
Ask for directions. Follow the arrows.

A: Excuse me. How do I get to the Empire State Building?
B: Walk up 42nd Street. Turn . . .

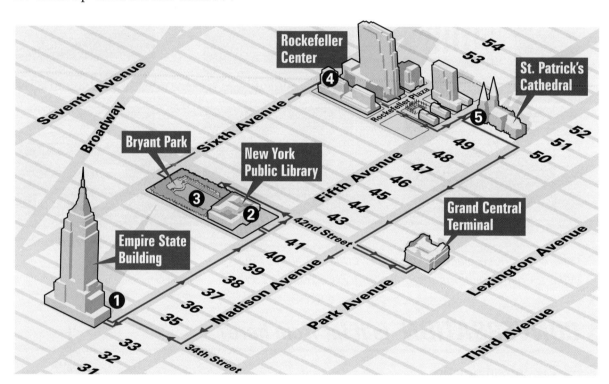

10 YOUR NEIGHBORHOOD

A Draw a map of your neighborhood.

B *Pair work* Look at your partner's map. Ask for directions
to places in your partner's neighborhood.

A: How do I get to the bookstore?
B: Walk . . .

11 INTERCHANGE 13 *Giving directions*

Give directions. Student A find Interchange 13A; Student B find Interchange 13B.

12 *READING* ⊙

A Walk Up Fifth Avenue

As you read, look at the map in Exercise 9.

1 Start your tour at the **Empire State Building** on Fifth Avenue between 33rd and 34th Streets. This building has 102 floors. Take the elevator to the 102nd floor for a great view of New York City.

2 Now walk up Fifth Avenue seven blocks to the **New York Public Library**. The entrance is between 40th and 42nd Streets. This library holds over 10 million books. Behind the library is **Bryant Park**. In the summer, there's an outdoor café, and at lunch hour, there are free music concerts.

3 Walk up Sixth Avenue to 49th Street. You're standing in the middle of the 19 buildings of **Rockefeller Center**. Turn right on 49th Street, walk another block, and turn left. You're in **Rockefeller Plaza**. In the winter, you can ice-skate in the rink there.

4 Right across from Rockefeller Center on Fifth Avenue is **St. Patrick's Cathedral**. It's modeled after the cathedral in Cologne, Germany. Go inside St. Patrick's and leave the noisy city behind. Look at the beautiful blue windows. Many of these windows come from France.

A Read the tourist information. Where can you . . . ?

1. listen to music outdoors ....
2. go ice-skating in the winter ....
3. sit quietly indoors ....
4. get a view of the city ....

B *Group work* Ask the questions in part A.
Answer with information about your city or town.

A: Where can you listen to music outdoors?
B: You can listen to music in the park next to the river.
C: Or you can . . .

14 Did you have fun?

SNAPSHOT

▶ Listen and practice.

Top Eight Things People Hate to Do

1. stand in line
2. do laundry
3. travel to work
4. go to meetings
5. exercise
6. work in the yard
7. clean the house
8. open the mail

Source: Based on information from *The Book of Lists*

Do you hate to do these things?
What other things do you hate to do? Why?

CONVERSATION *I didn't study!*

▶ Listen and practice.

Michael: Hi, Jennifer. Did you have a good weekend?
Jennifer: Well, I had a busy weekend, and I feel a little tired today.
Michael: Really? Why?
Jennifer: Well, on Saturday, I exercised in the morning. Then my roommate and I cleaned, did laundry, and shopped. And then I visited my parents.
Michael: So what did you do on Sunday?
Jennifer: I studied for the test all day.
Michael: Oh, no! Do we have a test today? I didn't study! I just watched television all weekend!

③ GRAMMAR FOCUS

Simple past statements: regular verbs ▶

							Spelling		
I	**studied**	on Sunday.	I	**didn't study**	on Saturday.		watch	→	watch**ed**
You	**watched**	television.	You	**didn't watch**	a movie.		exercise	→	exercis**ed**
She	**stayed**	home.	She	**didn't stay**	out.		study	→	stud**ied**
We	**shopped**	for groceries.	We	**didn't shop**	for clothes.		stay	→	stay**ed**
They	**exercised**	on Saturday.	They	**didn't exercise**	on Sunday.		shop	→	shop**ped**
				did**n't** = did not					

A Tim is talking about his weekend. Complete the sentences. Then compare with a partner.

On Friday night, I ....*waited*.... (wait) for a phone call, but my girlfriend ..*didn't call*.. (not call). I just .... (stay) home and .... (watch) television. On Saturday, I .... (visit) my friend Frank. We .... (talk) and .... (listen) to music. In the evening, he .... (invite) some friends over, and we .... (cook) a great meal. I .... (not work) very hard on Sunday. I .... (not study) at all. I just .... (walk) to the mall and .... (shop).

B Complete the sentences. Use your own information. Then compare with a partner.

1. Yesterday, I *watched / didn't watch* (watch) television.
2. Last night, I .... (stay) home.
3. Last week, I .... (exercise) every day.
4. Last month, I .... (shop) for clothes.
5. Last year, I .... (visit) a different country.

④ PRONUNCIATION Simple past -ed endings

A ▶ Listen and practice. Notice the pronunciation of **-ed**.

/t/	/d/	/ɪd/
work**ed**	clean**ed**	invit**ed**
watch**ed**	stay**ed**	visit**ed**
....	....	....
....	....	....

B ▶ Listen and write these verbs under the correct sounds.

cooked   exercised   listened   needed   shopped   waited

GRAMMAR FOCUS

Simple past statements: irregular verbs ▷

I **did** my homework.
I **didn't do** laundry.

You **got up** at noon.
You **didn't get up** at 10:00.

He **went** to the museum.
He **didn't go** to the library.

We **met** our classmates.
We **didn't meet** our teacher.

You **came** home late.
You **didn't come** home early.

They **had** a picnic.
They **didn't have** a party.

A ▷ Complete the chart. Then listen and check.

Present	Past	Present	Past	Present	Past
buy	bought	....	read /rɛd/	....	sat
....	ate	....	rode	....	took
....	felt	....	saw	....	wore

For a list of more irregular verbs, see the appendix at the back of the book.

B *Pair work* Did you do the things in the pictures yesterday? Tell your partner.

"Yesterday, I did my homework. I also did laundry. . . ."

6 LAST WEEKEND

A Write five things you *did* and five things you *didn't do* last weekend.

B *Group work* Tell your classmates about your weekend.

A: I saw a movie last weekend.
B: I didn't see a movie. But I watched television.
C: I watched television, too! I saw . . .

Things I did	Things I didn't do
I saw a movie.	I didn't exercise.
I studied.	I didn't buy clothes.

7 CONVERSATION *Did you like it?*

▶ Listen and practice.

Laura: So, did you go anywhere last summer?
Erica: Yes, I did. My sister and I went to Arizona. We saw the Grand Canyon.
Laura: Really? Did you like it?
Erica: Oh, yes. We loved it!
Laura: Did you go hiking there?
Erica: No, we didn't. Actually, we rode horses. And we also went white-water rafting on the Colorado River!
Laura: Wow! Did you have fun?
Erica: Yes, we did. We had a great time!

8 GRAMMAR FOCUS

Simple past yes/no questions ▷

Did you **have** a good summer?
    Yes, I **did**. I **had** a great summer.
Did you **play** volleyball?
    No, I **didn't**. I **played** tennis.

Did Erica **like** her vacation?
    Yes, she **did**. She **liked** it a lot.
Did Erica and her sister **go** to Colorado?
    No, they **didn't**. They **went** to Arizona.

A Complete the conversations. Then practice with a partner.

1. A: ...*Did*... you ...*have*... (have) a good summer?
   B: Yes, I .... I .... (have) a great summer. I just .... (relax).

2. A: .... you .... (go) anywhere last summer?
   B: No, I .... I .... (stay) here. But my friends .... (visit) me, and on the weekends we .... (go out) a lot.

3. A: .... you .... (take) any classes last summer?
   B: Yes, I .... I .... (take) tennis lessons, and I .... (play) tennis every day!

4. A: .... you .... (speak) English last summer?
   B: No, I .... But I .... (read) English books and I .... (watch) English movies.

B *Pair work* Ask the questions from part A. Answer with your own information.

A: Did you have a good summer?
B: No, I didn't. I just stayed home. . . .

9 LISTENING *I didn't go anywhere.*

Listen to Andy, Gail, Patrick, and Fran. What did they do last summer? Check (✓) the correct answers.

1. Andy   ☐ stayed home   ☑ visited his brother   ☐ went to the beach
2. Gail   ☐ saw movies   ☐ read books   ☐ watched television
3. Patrick   ☐ went bike riding   ☐ went jogging   ☐ played tennis
4. Fran   ☐ studied   ☐ had a job   ☐ painted the house

10 WORD POWER *Summer activities*

A Find two words from the list that go with each verb in the chart. Then listen and check.

a class   a picnic
fun   pictures
✓ hiking   a play
a movie   ✓ swimming
new people   tennis
old friends   volleyball

go	*hiking*	*swimming*
have		
meet		
play		
see		
take		

B *Pair work* Check (✓) six things to ask your partner. Then ask and answer questions.

Did you . . . last summer?

☐ go anywhere interesting   ☐ play any games
☐ buy anything interesting   ☐ read any books
☐ eat any new foods   ☐ see any movies
☐ meet any interesting people   ☐ take any pictures
☐ exercise or play any sports   ☐ wear different clothes
☐ work   ☐ have fun

A: Did you go anywhere interesting last summer?
B: Yes, I did. I went to the beach almost every day, and . . .

C *Class activity* Tell the class about your partner's summer.

"Last summer, Maria went to the beach almost every day. She . . ."

11 INTERCHANGE 14 *Past and present*

Are you different now from when you were a child? Go to Interchange 14.

WEEKEND STORIES

Scan the article. Who had a terrible weekend? Who enjoyed the weekend? Who learned a lot over the weekend?

Kelly

"I had a great weekend. I went to my best friend Helen's wedding. She got married at home. All her friends and family went. She looked fantastic! She wore a beautiful dress. After the ceremony, her parents served a wonderful meal. I'm really happy for her. And I really like her husband!"

Robert

"I had an awful weekend. My friends and I went to a rock concert. I had a terrible time! It took three hours to drive there. I didn't like the music at all! And after the concert ended, our car broke down! I called my parents, and they came and got us. We finally got home at ten this morning. I am so tired!"

Erin

"I had an interesting weekend. I went camping for the first time. My friends took me. We left on Saturday and drove to the campsite. First, we put up the tent. Then we built a fire, cooked dinner, and told stories. We got up early on Sunday and went fishing. I caught a fish! I didn't really like camping, but I learned a lot."

A Read the article. Then correct these sentences.

1. Kelly got married. *Kelly's best friend got married* .
2. Helen got married in a church. ....
3. After the wedding, everyone went out to eat. ....
4. Robert went to a rock concert with his parents. ....
5. It took three hours to get home after the concert. ....
6. Robert got home at ten o'clock last night. ....
7. Erin goes camping every weekend. ....
8. Erin and her friends went fishing on Saturday. ....
9. Erin liked camping a lot. ....

B *Group work* Do you have a story about a wedding, rock concert, or camping trip? Write four sentences about it. Then tell your classmates.

Units 13-14 Progress check

SELF-ASSESSMENT

How well can you do these things? Check (✓) the boxes.

I can	Very well	OK	A little
Listen to and understand conversations about places and things (Ex. 1)	☐	☐	☐
Ask and answer questions about places using prepositions of place (Ex. 2)	☐	☐	☐
Ask for and give directions (Ex. 2)	☐	☐	☐
Talk about your last vacation using simple past (Ex. 3)	☐	☐	☐
Ask and answer simple past yes/no questions about last weekend (Ex. 4)	☐	☐	☐

1 LISTENING What are you looking for?

▶ Listen to the conversations. What do the people need?
Where can they get or find it? Complete the chart.

What	Where
1.	....
2.	....
3.	....
4.	....

2 WHERE IS THE . . . ?

A *Pair work* Are these places near your school? Where are they?
Ask and answer questions.

bank	coffee shop	hospital	post office
bookstore	department store	park	supermarket

A: Where is the bank?
B: It's on Second Avenue. It's across from the Korean restaurant.

B *Pair work* Give directions from your school to the places in part A.
Your partner guesses the place.

A: Walk up First Avenue and turn left. It's on the right, on the corner
  of First and Lincoln.
B: It's the coffee shop.
A: That's right!

98

MY LAST VACATION

A Write four statements about your last vacation.
Two are true and two are false.

> I went to London.
> I saw a play.
> I didn't take any pictures.
> I didn't go to a museum.

B *Pair work* Read your statements. Your partner says
"True" or "False." Who has more correct guesses?

A: On my last vacation, I went to London.
B: False.
A: That's right. It's false. OR Sorry. It's true.

 LAST WEEKEND

A Check (✓) the things you did last weekend.
Then add two more things you did.

☐ saw a movie	☐ had dinner at a restaurant
☐ worked in the yard	☐ read a book
☐ cleaned the house	☐ went dancing
☐ exercised or played sports	☐ met some interesting people
☐ went shopping	☐ talked on the phone
☐ bought some clothes	☐ got up late
☐ saw friends	☐ ....
☐ studied	☐ ....

B *Pair work* Ask your partner about his or her weekend.

A: Did you see a movie last weekend, Keiko?
B: Yes, I did. I saw the new Tom Cruise movie.
 I loved it. Did you see a movie?
A: No, I didn't. . . .

C *Group work* Join another pair. Tell them about
your partner's weekend.

"Keiko saw the new Tom Cruise movie. She loved it. . . ."

WHAT'S NEXT?

Look at your Self-assessment again. Do you need to review anything?

15 Where were you born?

1 SNAPSHOT

▶ Listen and practice.

WHERE WERE THESE PEOPLE BORN?

1. ____
2. ____
3. ____
4. ____
5. ____

Issey Miyake, designer

Shakira, singer

Chow Yun Fat, actor

Salma Hayek, actress

Ronaldo, athlete

a. Brazil
b. China
c. Colombia
d. Japan
e. Mexico

Answers: 1. d   2. c   3. b   4. e   5. a

Sources: *www.biography.com; www.celebrities.net.cn; www.salma.com*

Match the people with the countries. Then check your answers at the bottom of the Snapshot.
What famous people were born in your country? What do they do?

2 CONVERSATION *I was born in Korea.*

▶ Listen and practice.

Chuck: Where were you born, Melissa?
Melissa: I was born in Korea.
Chuck: Oh! So you weren't born in the U.S.
Melissa: No, I came here in 1999.
Chuck: Hmm. You were pretty young.
Melissa: Yes, I was only seventeen.
Chuck: Did you go to college right away?
Melissa: No, my English wasn't very good, so I took English classes for two years first.
Chuck: Well, your English is really good now.
Melissa: Thanks. Your English is pretty good, too.
Chuck: Yeah, but I was born here.

3 GRAMMAR FOCUS

Statements with the past of be ▶

I **was** born in Korea.	I **wasn't** born in the U.S.	**Contractions**
You **were** pretty young.	You **weren't** very old.	wasn't = was not
She **was** seventeen.	She **wasn't** in college.	weren't = were not
We **were** born in the same year.	We **weren't** born in the same country.	
They **were** in Korea in 1998.	They **weren't** in the U.S. in 1998.	

A Melissa is talking about her family. Choose the correct verb forms. Then compare with a partner.

My family and I ..*were*.. (was / were) all born in Korea – we .... (wasn't / weren't) born in the U.S. I .... (was / were) born in the city of Inchon, and my brother .... (was / were) born there, too. My parents .... (wasn't / weren't) born in Inchon. They .... (was / were) born in the capital, Seoul.

Seoul

Questions with the past of be ▶

Were you born in the U.S.?
  Yes, I **was**.
  No, I **wasn't**.
Was your brother born in 1984?
  Yes, he **was**.
  No, he **wasn't**.
Were your parents born in Inchon?
  Yes, they **were**.
  No, they **weren't**.

Where were you born?
  I **was** born in Korea.

When was he born?
  He **was** born in 1985.

What city were they born **in**?
  They **were** born in Seoul.

B Complete these questions with *was* or *were*.

1. ..*Were*.. you born in this city?
2. When .... you born?
3. Where .... your parents born?
4. When .... your mother born?
5. When .... your father born?
6. .... you and your family in this city last year?
7. .... you at this school last year?
8. Who .... your first English teacher?
9. What nationality .... your first English teacher?
10. What .... he or she like?

years ▶

1906 (nineteen oh six)
1917 (nineteen seventeen)
1999 (nineteen ninety-nine)
2001 (two thousand and one)

C *Pair work* Ask and answer the questions from part B. Use your own information.

A: Were you born in this city?
B: No, I wasn't. I was born in Tokyo.

LISTENING *Where was she born?*

 Where were these people born? When were they born?
Listen and complete the chart.

Michelle Yeoh

Apolo Ohno

Gisele Bündchen

Gael García Bernal

	Place of birth	Year of birth
1. Michelle Yeoh	*Malaysia*	
2. Apolo Ohno		
3. Gisele Bündchen		
4. Gael García Bernal		

5 *PRONUNCIATION* Negative contractions

A Listen and practice.

one syllable	two syllables
aren't don't	isn't doesn't
weren't can't	wasn't didn't

B Listen and practice.

They **didn't** eat dinner because they **weren't** hungry.
I **don't** like coffee, and she **doesn't** like tea.
These **aren't** their swimsuits. They **can't** swim.
He **wasn't** here yesterday, and he **isn't** here today.

C Write four sentences with negative contractions.
Then read them to a partner.

I didn't go because my friends weren't there.

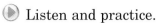

6 CONVERSATION *Where did you grow up?*

Listen and practice.

Melissa: So, Chuck, where did you grow up?
Chuck: I grew up in Texas. I was born there, too.
Melissa: And when did you come to Los Angeles?
Chuck: In 1990. I went to college here.
Melissa: Oh. What was your major?
Chuck: Drama. I was an actor for five years after college.
Melissa: That's interesting. So why did you become a hairstylist?
Chuck: Because I needed the money. And I love it. Look. What do you think?
Melissa: Well, uh . . .

7 GRAMMAR FOCUS

Wh-questions with did, was, *and* were

Where did you grow up?	I **grew up** in Texas.
When did you come to Los Angeles?	I **came** to Los Angeles in 1990.
Why did you become a hairstylist?	Because I **needed** the money.
How old were you in 1990?	I **was** eighteen.
What was your major in college?	It **was** drama.
How was college?	It **was** great.

A Match the questions with the answers. Then compare with a partner.

1. When and where were you born? ...c...
2. Where did you grow up? ....
3. When did you start school? ....
4. How old were you then? ....
5. How was your first day of school? ....
6. Who was your first friend in school? ....
7. What was he/she like? ....
8. Why did you take this class? ....

a. I was six.
b. She was really shy.
c. I was born in 1983 in Hiroshima, Japan.
d. Her name was Yumiko.
e. My English wasn't very good.
f. I grew up in Tokyo.
g. I entered first grade in 1989.
h. It was a little scary.

B *Pair work* Ask and answer the questions in part A. Use your own information.

8 WORD POWER

A ▶ Complete the word map with words from the list. Then listen and check.

✓ classroom
college
elementary
gym
high
history
junior high
lunchroom
math
physical education
playground
science

School days

Classes
....
....
....
....

Schools
....
....
....
....

Places
classroom
....
....
....

B *Pair work* Find out about your partner's elementary, junior high, or high school days. Ask these questions. Then tell the class.

What classes did you take?	Who was your favorite teacher? Why?
What was your favorite class? Why?	Who was your least favorite teacher? Why?
What was your least favorite class? Why?	Where did you spend your free time? Why?
Who was your best friend?	What did you like best?

"In elementary school, Dan spent his free time in the gym because he played a lot of sports. . . ."

9 FIRST DAY OF CLASS

A *Group work* Do you remember the first day of this class? Ask and answer these questions.

1. What did you wear?
2. Were you early, late, or on time?
3. Where did you sit?
4. How did you feel?
5. Who was the first person you met?
6. What did the teacher talk about?
7. Who talked the most? the least?
8. How was your English then? How is it now?

B *Class activity* What does your group remember? Tell the class.

10 INTERCHANGE 15 Time line

Make a time line of your life. Go to Interchange 15.

RICKY MARTIN

> **Scan the article. What three cities did Ricky Martin live in?**

Ricky Martin was born in San Juan, Puerto Rico, on December 24, 1971. He was always a performer. As a child, he appeared in television commercials and studied singing.

At the age of 12, he joined the Latin boy band, Menudo. He worked hard with them, and he became very well known. But he left the group after five years.

Martin moved to New York City, but he didn't work for a year. He was very frustrated, so he moved to Mexico City and got a part on a Mexican soap opera. Soon afterward, he recorded two Spanish-language albums. After this success, he moved back to the U.S.

Back in the U.S., he appeared on an American soap opera and in the Broadway show, *Les Miserables*. Then he made his first English-language album.

That album was called *Ricky Martin*. His biggest hit, "Livin' La Vida Loca," was on that album.

Now he's famous around the world. But he still works hard, and he still loves singing. As he said to a reporter for the newspaper *USA Today*: "I want to do this forever."

A Read the article. Then write a question for each answer.

1. .... ?	In Puerto Rico.
2. .... ?	At the age of 12.
3. .... ?	After five years.
4. .... ?	Because he was frustrated.
5. .... ?	*Les Miserables*.
6. .... ?	"Livin' La Vida Loca."

B Number these events in Ricky Martin's life from 1 (first event) to 10 (last event).

.... a. He joined a boy band.
.... b. He moved to New York City.
.... c. He made an English-language album.
.... d. He appeared in a Broadway musical.
.... e. He recorded albums in Spanish.

..1.. g. He was born.
.... f. He returned to the U.S.
.... h. He left Menudo.
.... i. He studied singing.
.... j. He moved to Mexico.

C *Group work* Who is your favorite singer? What do you know about his or her life? Tell your classmates.

16 Can she call you later?

1 CONVERSATION *I was in the shower.*

▶ Listen and practice.

Answering
machine: Hi. This is Jennifer, and this is Nicole.
We can't come to the phone right now.
Please leave us a message after the tone.
Michael: Hi. This is Michael. . . .
Nicole: Oh, hi, Michael. It's Nicole. Sorry I didn't
answer the phone right away. I was in
the shower.
Michael: That's OK. Is Jennifer there?
Nicole: No, she's at the mall. Can she call you later?
Michael: Yeah, thanks. Please ask her to call me
at home.
Nicole: Sure.
Michael: Thanks a lot, Nicole.

2 WORD POWER *Prepositional phrases*

A ▶ Listen and practice.

at home	**at the** mall	**in** bed	**in the** shower	**on** vacation
at work	**at the** library	**in** class	**in the** hospital	**on** a trip
at school	**at the** beach	**in** Mexico	**in the** yard	**on** his/her break

at the mall

in class

on vacation

B *Pair work* Make a list of five friends and family members.
Give it to your partner. Where are these people right now?
Ask and answer questions.

A: Where's your brother right now?
B: He's on vacation. He's in Thailand.

LISTENING *She's in the yard.*

A ▶ Listen to people call Lisa, Jeff, Brenda, and Eric. Where are they? Complete the sentences.

1. Lisa is *in the yard* . 3. Brenda is ....
2. Jeff is .... 4. Eric is ....

B *Pair work* Call the people in part A.

A: Hello. Is Lisa there, please?
B: Yes, but she's in the yard.

GRAMMAR FOCUS

> **Subject and object pronouns** ▶

Subjects		Objects
I		me
You		you
He		him
She got Michael's message.	Michael left	**her** a message.
We		us
They		them

A Complete the phone conversations with the correct pronouns. Then practice with a partner.

1. A: Can .....*I*..... speak with Ms. Fee, please?
   B: ....'s not here. But maybe .... can help you.
   A: Please give .... my new phone number. It's 555-2981.

2. A: Hi, this is David. Is Mr. Roberts there?
   B: .... 'm sorry, but .... 's not here right now.
      Do you want to leave .... a message?
   A: Yes. Please tell .... to call me at work.

3. A: Hello, this is Carol's Café. Are Kate and Joe in?
   B: No, ...'re not. Can .... help you?
   A: .... found Kate and Joe's keys. .... left .... on the table.
   B: Just bring .... the keys. I can give .... to Kate and Joe.
   A: I'm sorry, but .... can't. Can Kate and Joe call .... ?
   B: OK.

B Write messages for three classmates. Then call a partner and leave each classmate a message.

A: Hello. Is Yuko in?
B: I'm sorry. She's at the library. Can I take a message?
A: Yes. Please tell her to meet me after class.

> *Yuko — Meet me*
> *after class.*

5 SNAPSHOT

▶ Listen and practice.

Popular Activities in the U.S.

☐ go to the movies

☐ go to a concert

☐ visit an amusement park

☐ see a sports event

☐ go to an art festival

Sources: *The Encyclopedia Britannica*; The National Endowment for the Arts

Check (✓) the activities that are popular in your country.
What other activities are popular in your country?
What are your favorite activities? Why?

6 CONVERSATION *I'd love to!*

▶ Listen and practice.

Michael: Hello?
Jennifer: Hi, Michael. It's Jennifer. I got your message.
Michael: Hi. Thanks for calling me back.
Jennifer: So, what's up?
Michael: Uh, well, do you want to see a movie with me tomorrow night?
Jennifer: Tomorrow night? I'm sorry, but I can't. I have to study for a test.
Michael: Oh, that's too bad. How about Friday night?
Jennifer: Uh, . . . sure. I'd love to. What time do you want to meet?
Michael: How about around seven o'clock?
Jennifer: Terrific!

7 PRONUNCIATION Want to *and* have to

A ▶ Listen and practice. Notice the reduction of **want to** and **have to**.

/wanə/
A: Do you **want to** go to a party with me tonight?

/hæftə/
B: I'm sorry, I can't. I **have to** work late.

B *Pair work* Practice the conversation in Exercise 6 again. Try to reduce **want to** and **have to**.

go to a party

8 GRAMMAR FOCUS

> **Invitations; verb + to**
>
> **Do you want to see** a movie with me tonight?
> Sure. I'**d** really **like to** see a good comedy.
> I'**d like** to (see a movie), but I **have to** study.
> I'**d** = I would
>
> **Would you like to go** to a soccer game?
> Yes, I'**d love to** (go to a soccer game)!
> I **want to** (go), but I **need to** work.

A Complete the invitations. Then match them with the responses.

Invitations

1. Would you ...*like to*... visit an amusement park this weekend? ...*d*...

2. Do you .... go to a basketball game tomorrow night? ....

3. Would you .... see a movie tonight? ....

4. Do you .... go swimming on Saturday? ....

5. Do you .... play soccer after school today? ....

6. Would you .... go to an art festival on Sunday afternoon? ....

Responses

a. I'd like to, but I don't have a swimsuit!

b. I'm sorry, but I have to talk to the teacher after school.

c. I don't really like basketball. Do you want to do something else?

d. I'd like to, but I can't. I'm going to go on a trip this weekend.

e. Yes, I'd love to. I love art festivals!

f. Tonight? I can't. I need to help my parents.

B *Pair work* Practice the invitations from part A. Respond with your own information.

A: Do you want to go to a basketball game tomorrow night?
B: I'd like to, but I can't. I have to work. . . .

Can she call you later? • **109**

9 EXCUSES, EXCUSES!

A Do you ever use these excuses? Check (✓) Often, Sometimes, or Never. What are your three favorite excuses? Compare with a partner.

	Often	Sometimes	Never
I have to babysit.	☐	☐	☐
I need to study for a test.	☐	☐	☐
I have to work late.	☐	☐	☐
I need to go to bed early.	☐	☐	☐
I want to visit my family.	☐	☐	☐
I have a class.	☐	☐	☐
I have a headache.	☐	☐	☐
I'm not feeling well.	☐	☐	☐
I need to do laundry.	☐	☐	☐
I already have plans.	☐	☐	☐

I have to babysit.

B Write down three things you want to do this weekend.

I want to go to the baseball game on Saturday.

C *Class activity* Go around the class and invite your classmates to do the things from part B. Your classmates respond with excuses.

A: Would you like to go to the baseball game on Saturday?
B: I'm sorry, but I can't. I have to . . .

10 LISTENING I'd love to, but . . .

A 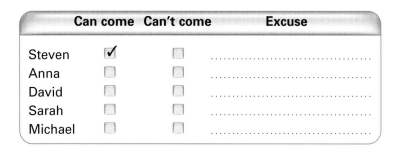 Jennifer and Nicole invited some people to a party. Listen to their answering machine messages. Who can come? Who can't come? Check (✓) the correct answers.

	Can come	Can't come	Excuse
Steven	✔	☐	....
Anna	☐	☐	....
David	☐	☐	....
Sarah	☐	☐	....
Michael	☐	☐	....

B Listen again. Why can't some people come? Write their excuses.

11 INTERCHANGE 16 Let's make a date!

Make a date with your classmates. Go to Interchange 16.

MIAMI *Florida* — What's on This Saturday?

Look at the shows and events. Which do you want to go to? Number the pictures from 1 (most interesting) to 5 (least interesting).

IMAX Movie at the Museum of Discovery and Science

Shows at 4, 6, 8, and 10 P.M.

Do you want to travel, but don't have the money? Experience the world through the IMAX movie *The Greatest Places*. Seats in the theater sell out fast, so come early!

Animal Shows at Parrot Jungle Island

Open 10:00 A.M. to 6:00 P.M.

There are over 3,000 exotic animals and 100 plants at this beautiful nature park. Amazing animal tricks and outdoor animal shows, too.

Rock Concert on South Beach

7:00 P.M. to midnight

Come hear some great music under the stars! Five terrific bands are going to play. Sandwiches and soda sold.

Summer Fashion Show at Dolphin Mall

Starts at 3:00 P.M.

Men's and women's summer clothes. Seating is still available to see the latest fashions. All clothing is on sale after the show for under $100.

Art Festival at Broward Community College

9:00 A.M. to 5:00 P.M.

Need to buy a present? Check out this multicultural event. Find jewelry, paintings, clothing, and more! Food from around the world, too.

 Home   **Map**   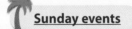 **Sunday events**    **Contact us**

A Read the Web page. Where can you do these things? Write two places.

1. buy clothes or jewelry ....
2. buy food ....
3. sit indoors ....
4. be outdoors ....
5. see a live performance ....

B *Group work* Where do you like to go in your city or town? What shows or events do you like? Tell your classmates.

Units 15–16 Progress check

SELF-ASSESSMENT

How well can you do these things? Check (✓) the boxes.

I can	Very well	OK	A little
Talk about your past using the past of *be* (Ex. 1)	☐	☐	☐
Ask about famous people using simple past yes/no questions (Ex. 2)	☐	☐	☐
Listen to and understand phone calls with subject and object pronouns (Ex. 3)	☐	☐	☐
Ask yes/no questions using verb + *to* (Ex. 4, 5)	☐	☐	☐
Make, accept, and refuse invitations (Ex. 5)	☐	☐	☐
Give excuses (Ex. 5)	☐	☐	☐

1 WHERE WERE YOU IN . . . ?

A *Pair work* Choose three years in your partner's life. Then ask your partner the questions and complete the chart.

	199___	199___	200___
How old were you in . . . ?	....	....	....
Where were you in . . . ?	....	....	....
What were you like in . . . ?	....	....	....

B *Class activity* Tell the class about your partner's life.

"In 1990, Raul was four. He . . ."

2 WHO WAS HE?

Group work Think of a famous person from the past. Your classmates ask yes/no questions to guess the person.

Was he/she born in . . . ?
Was he/she a singer? an actor?
Was he/she tall? heavy? good-looking?

A: I'm thinking of a famous man from the past.
B: Was he born in the U.S.?
A: No, he wasn't.
C: Was he . . . ?

LISTENING *On the phone*

 Listen and check (✓) the best response.

1. ☐ Yes. Please tell her to call me.
   ☐ Yes. Please tell him to call me.

2. ☐ Yes. Does he have your number?
   ☐ No. He isn't here right now.

3. ☐ Yes, you do.
   ☐ No, I don't.

4. ☐ I'm going to visit my parents.
   ☐ I had a terrible headache.

5. ☐ I'm sorry, but I can't go.
   ☐ No, I didn't go. I was at work.

6. ☐ I'm sorry, he's not here right now.
   ☐ No, Sandra is at work right now.

FIND SOMEONE WHO . . .

A *Class activity* Go around the class. Ask questions to complete the chart. Try to write a different name on each line.

Find someone who	Name
needs to do laundry this weekend	....
doesn't want to do homework tonight	....
has to babysit this week	....
would like to go shopping this weekend	....
wants to see a movie tonight	....
has to go to the doctor this week	....
needs to work this weekend	....
would like to go home early	....

A: Megumi, do you need to do laundry this weekend?
B: Yes, I do.

B *Pair work* Compare your answers with a partner.

INVITATIONS

A Make a list of five things you want to do this summer.

B *Class activity* Go around the class. Invite your classmates to do the things from part A. Your classmates accept or refuse the invitations.

A: Would you like to play tennis this summer?
B: I'm sorry, I can't. I have to . . . .

C: Do you want to go to an art festival this summer?
D: Sure, I'd love to! When would you like to . . . ?

WHAT'S NEXT?

Look at your Self-assessment again. Do you need to review anything?

Interchange activities

FOOD SURVEY

A Complete the food survey. Use these foods and other foods you know.

Things I	eat every day	eat twice a week	eat once a week	never eat
meat/fish				
dairy				
fruits				
vegetables				
snacks				

B *Pair work* Compare your information.

A: I eat onions every day.
B: I never eat onions, but I eat chocolates every day.

Interchange 9

A *Class activity* Go around the class. Find someone who *can* and someone who *can't* do each thing. Try to write a different name on each line.

Can you . . . ?	Names	
	Can	**Can't**
play three musical instruments	....	....
dance the tango	....	....
say "Hello" in five languages	....	....
swim underwater	....	....
write with both hands	....	....
do a handstand	....	....
fix a computer	....	....
juggle	....	....
sew your own clothes	....	....
do magic tricks	....	....

dance the tango

write with both hands

do a handstand

juggle

sew your own clothes

do magic tricks

A: Can you play three musical instruments?
B: Yes, I can. OR No, I can't.

B *Class activity* Share your answers with the class.

"Mei-Li can't play three musical instruments, but Claudia can.
She can play the guitar, violin, and piano."

A *Pair work* Is your partner going to do any of these things? Check (✓) your guesses.

Is your partner going to . . . ?	My guesses		My partner's answers	
	Yes	No	Yes	No
1. watch television tonight	☐	☐	☐	☐
2. study English this evening	☐	☐	☐	☐
3. use a computer tomorrow	☐	☐	☐	☐
4. cook dinner tomorrow night	☐	☐	☐	☐
5. go out with friends this weekend	☐	☐	☐	☐
6. eat at a restaurant this weekend	☐	☐	☐	☐
7. go to the gym next week	☐	☐	☐	☐
8. buy something expensive this month	☐	☐	☐	☐
9. go on a trip next month	☐	☐	☐	☐
10. visit family next summer	☐	☐	☐	☐

B *Pair work* Ask and answer questions to check your guesses.

A: Are you going to watch television tonight?
B: Yes, I am. I'm going to watch a movie.

C *Class activity* How many of your guesses are correct?
Who has the most correct guesses?

GIVING DIRECTIONS

Student A

A *Pair work* Look at the map. You are on Third Avenue between
Maple and Oak Streets. Ask your partner for directions to these places.
(There are no signs for these places on your map.) Then label the buildings.

garage   supermarket   flower shop

A: Excuse me. How do I get to the garage?
B: Walk down Third Avenue to . . .

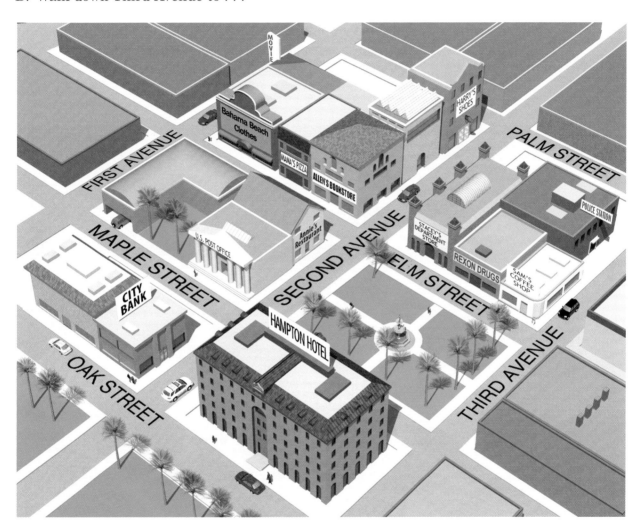

B *Pair work* Your partner asks you for directions to three places.
(There are signs for these places on your map.) Use the expressions
in the box to give directions.

Go up/Go down . . .	It's on the corner of . . . Street and . . . Avenue.	It's next to . . .
Walk up/Walk down . . .		It's behind . . .
Turn right/Turn left . . .	It's between . . . and . . .	It's in front of . . .
	It's across from . . .	

Student B

A *Pair work* Look at the map. You are on Third Avenue between Maple and Oak Streets. Your partner asks you for directions to three places. (There are signs for these places on your map.) Use the expressions in the box to give directions.

A: Excuse me. How do I get to the garage?
B: Walk down Third Avenue to . . .

Go up/Go down . . .	It's on the corner of . . . Street	It's next to . . .
Walk up/Walk down . . .	and . . . Avenue.	It's behind . . .
Turn right/Turn left . . .	It's between . . . and . . .	It's in front of . . .
	It's across from . . .	

B *Pair work* Ask your partner for directions to these places.
(There are no signs for these places on your map.) Then label the buildings.

coffee shop   shoe store   bookstore

A *Pair work* Imagine you have these problems. Your partner gives advice.

I can't lose weight. I really like dessert. Cake is my favorite food!

1

My job is very stressful. I usually work 10 hours a day and on weekends.

2

I can never get up on time in the morning. I'm always late for school.

3

I'm new in town, and I don't know any people here. How can I make some friends?

4

It's my best friend's birthday, and I don't have a present for her. All the stores are closed!

5

I have a big test tomorrow. My family is very noisy, and I can't study!

6

A: I can't lose weight. . . .
B: Exercise every day. And . . .

B *Class activity* Think of two problems you have.
Then tell the class. Your classmates give advice.

A: I don't understand this activity.
B: Read the instructions again.
C: Don't worry! Ask the teacher.

PAST AND PRESENT

A *Pair work* Ask your partner questions about his or her past and present. Check (✓) the answers.

A: Did you clean your room as a child?
B: Yes, I did. OR No, I didn't.

A: Do you clean your room now?
B: Yes, I do. OR No, I don't.

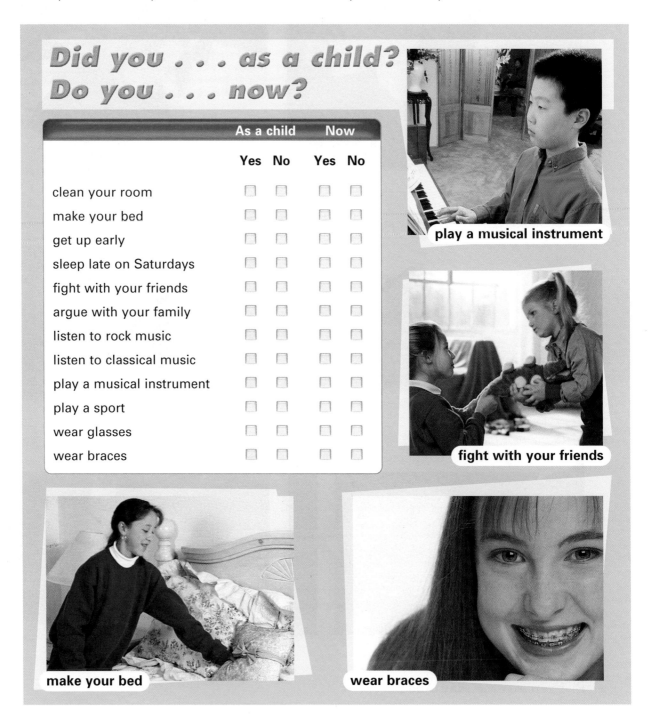

Did you . . . as a child?
Do you . . . now?

	As a child		Now	
	Yes	No	Yes	No
clean your room	☐	☐	☐	☐
make your bed	☐	☐	☐	☐
get up early	☐	☐	☐	☐
sleep late on Saturdays	☐	☐	☐	☐
fight with your friends	☐	☐	☐	☐
argue with your family	☐	☐	☐	☐
listen to rock music	☐	☐	☐	☐
listen to classical music	☐	☐	☐	☐
play a musical instrument	☐	☐	☐	☐
play a sport	☐	☐	☐	☐
wear glasses	☐	☐	☐	☐
wear braces	☐	☐	☐	☐

play a musical instrument

fight with your friends

make your bed

wear braces

B *Group work* Join another pair. Tell them about changes in your partner's life.

"Paulo didn't clean his room as a child, but he cleans his room now."

LIFE EVENTS

A What were five important events in your life? Mark the years and events on the time line. Then write a sentence about each one.

I was born . . .

I got a bicycle . . .

I started elementary school . . .

I graduated from high school . . .

I moved to a new place . . .

I won a prize . . .

I fell in love . . .

I got married . . .

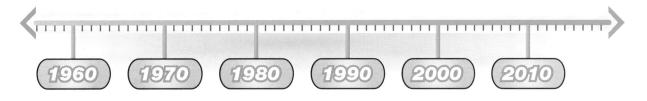

1960   1970   1980   1990   2000   2010

1. *I was born in 1984.* ....

2. ....

3. ....

4. ....

5. ....

B *Pair work* Ask your partner about his or her time line.

A: What happened in 2003?
B: I fell in love.
A: How old were you?
B: I was twenty-three.

A Imagine this is next month's calendar. Write ten plans on
the calendar. Use these expressions and your own ideas.

go to (the movies/a party)	play (tennis/basketball)
go (dancing/shopping)	meet (my friend/teacher)
go on vacation	have dinner with (my brother/parents)
study for (a test/an exam)	visit (my parents/grandparents)
go out with (my girlfriend/boyfriend)	see (the dentist/doctor)

SUNDAY	MONDAY	TUESDAY	WEDNESDAY	THURSDAY	FRIDAY	SATURDAY
1	2	3	4	5	6	7
8	9	10	11	12	13	14
15	16	17	18	19	20	21
22	23	24	25	26	27	28
29	30	31				

B *Group work* Look at your calendars. Agree on a date to do
something together.

A: Do you want to do something on March third?
B: I'd like to, but I can't. I'm going to play volleyball. How about
   March fourth?
C: March fourth? Sorry, I have to . . .

C *Group work* Make a plan to do something together. Then share
your plans with the class.

A: We can all do something on March seventh. Would you like to play tennis?
B: No, I don't play tennis very well. Do you want to go to a museum?
C: Well, I really don't like museums. . . .

Units 9–16 Self-study

9 PARTY MENU

A Listen to Sue and Fred talk about foods for a party.
Number the foods from 1 to 8.

B Listen again. Cross out the foods Sue and Fred don't get.

cake	crackers and cheese	~~hamburgers~~	soda
cookies	fruit	potato chips	vegetables

10 SPORTS AND ACTIVITIES

A Listen to the conversations. Number the pictures from 1 to 4.

B Listen again. Check (✓) the questions you hear.

1. ☐ What sports do you play?
   ☐ What sports do you watch?

2. ☐ What time do you practice?
   ☐ How often do you practice?

3. ☐ When do you practice?
   ☐ Who do you practice with?

4. ☐ Where do you play?
   ☐ When do you play?

11 A BUSY SUMMER

A ▶ Listen to Jill and Kenny's conversation. Write the dates for each event.

Event	Date	What are they going to do?
John's graduation	June 15th	have a party
Amy and Jeff's wedding		
Parents' anniversary		
Kenny's birthday		

B ▶ Listen again. How are they going to celebrate each event? Complete the chart.

12 HEALTH TALK

A ▶ Listen. What is a different way to say each sentence or question? Number these sentences or questions from 1 to 6.

.... Go to bed early.   .... I have a stomachache.   .... I don't feel well.
...1... How do you feel?   .... My eyes are sore.   .... What's wrong?

B ▶ Listen again. Check (✓) the best response.

1. ☑ I'm just fine, thanks.
   ☐ What's wrong?

2. ☐ That's good.
   ☐ Maybe I can help.

3. ☐ I feel better.
   ☐ I have a cold.

4. ☐ Take some antacid.
   ☐ Buy some aspirin.

5. ☐ That's good advice.
   ☐ I don't think so.

6. ☐ I'm sorry to hear that.
   ☐ Try some cough drops.

13 WHERE IS IT?

A ▶ Listen. Where do the people want to go? Number the pictures from 1 to 4.

B ▶ Listen again. Where are the places? Correct the mistakes.

1. It's on Center Street, ~~across from~~ *between* the drugstore and the gas station.

2. It's on Main Street, next to the department store.

3. It's on the corner of Center Avenue and First Street, across from the hotel.

4. It's on the corner of Center Avenue and Fourth Street, across from the drugstore.

14 LAST WEEKEND

A ▶ Listen to the conversations. Did Gary, Debra, and Brian have good weekends? Check (✓) Yes or No.

Gary   ☐ Yes   ☐ No   Debra   ☐ Yes   ☐ No   Brian   ☐ Yes   ☐ No

B ▶ Listen again. Put each person's activities in time order from 1 to 4.

Gary	**Debra**	**Brian** . . . .
.... had a party	.... did laundry	.... met friends
.... cooked food	.... shopped for groceries	.... played volleyball
..*1*.. played basketball	.... studied for a test	.... went swimming
.... watched a movie	.... cleaned the house	.... had a picnic

15 TIME LINE

A ▶ Listen to an interview with an actress. Write the years you hear on the time line.

1983

B ▶ Listen again. Complete the sentences with the correct years.

1. The actress was born in ...*1983*... .
2. She graduated from high school in ....
3. She got her first acting job in ....
4. She moved to the U.S. in ....
5. She started acting in ....
6. She was in her first movie in ....

16 HI, KATE!

▶ Listen. There are three mistakes in each message. Correct the mistakes.

1. Hi, Kate! This is Don. My ~~brother~~ *sister* is visiting me, and we're going to see a movie tomorrow night. Do you want to come? Please call me by 5:00 today.

2. Hi, Kate. This is Bill. Sorry I missed your call. I was in the yard. I'd love to have lunch with you tomorrow, but I can't. I have to study for a test. Sorry!

3. Hi, Kate. This is Howard. I was in Mexico last week, so I missed our math class. What did we study? Please call me at home. The number is 555-4509. Thanks.

Self-study audio scripts

9 Party menu

A Listen to Sue and Fred talk about foods for a party. Number the foods from 1 to 8.

SUE: What do you want for the party? We don't have any food – and the party is tomorrow!
FRED: Hmm. How about hamburgers?
SUE: Oh, I don't want hamburgers. Let's just have snacks.
FRED: Like what?
SUE: How about some crackers and cheese?
FRED: Good idea! I love crackers and cheese! And let's get some potato chips.
SUE: Hmm. I don't really want potato chips. They aren't very good for you. I know! Let's have some vegetables. How about carrots and celery?
FRED: Oh, no. I don't want any carrots and celery. People hardly ever eat vegetables at parties.
SUE: OK, then. No carrots and celery. But let's get some fresh fruit. Everyone likes fruit. Maybe strawberries and mangoes?
FRED: Yeah, I like strawberries and mangoes. . . . And we need dessert. I know! Let's get some cake.
SUE: No, cake is too difficult to eat. Let's get some cookies.
FRED: Oh, OK. Anything else?
SUE: Oh, yeah! Do we need any drinks?
FRED: Yeah, we do. Let's get some soda.
SUE: I think that's it. Now let's make a shopping list.

B Listen again. Cross out the foods Sue and Fred don't get.

10 Sports and activities

A Listen to the conversations. Number the pictures from 1 to 4.

1. WOMAN: Do you play any sports?
   MAN: No, I don't. But I like to watch sports.
   WOMAN: What sports do you watch?
   MAN: Hockey. It's always exciting!

2. WOMAN: Wow! I didn't know you can play the violin.
   MAN: Yes. I can play pretty well.
   WOMAN: How often do you practice?
   MAN: Every day.

3. MAN: I love tennis. I play almost every day.
   WOMAN: When do you practice?
   MAN: I practice at 6:30 A.M.
   WOMAN: Six-thirty in the morning? That's early!

4. MAN: Can you play chess?
   WOMAN: Yes, I can. I'm on the chess team at school.
   MAN: Great. Where do you play?
   WOMAN: We usually play in a classroom.

B Listen again. Check the questions you hear.

11 A busy summer

A Listen to Jill and Kenny's conversation. Write the dates for each event.

JILL: This summer is going to be busy.
KENNY: You're right! John's graduation is on June 15th.
JILL: Yes. And Amy and Jeff's wedding is just a week later. On June 22nd.
KENNY: Are we going to have a party for John's graduation?
JILL: Yes, remember? We're going to have a party for all his friends.
KENNY: Oh, yeah. And what about Amy and Jeff's wedding?
JILL: Oh, yes, on June 22nd. Well, I know we're going to give them a present . . . Then, look here. Our parents' anniversary is the next month.
KENNY: Oh, right. When is it again?
JILL: On July 10th. Don't you remember?
KENNY: Right, right. July 10th. So what are we going to do? Are we going to have a party?
JILL: No, I don't think they want a party. I think they want to go out for dinner in a nice restaurant. And what are we going to celebrate on August 9th?
KENNY: My birthday! August 9th is my birthday!
JILL: So, how are we going to celebrate?
KENNY: Are we going to have a picnic? I want to have a picnic!
JILL: That sounds fun.
KENNY: Yeah! It's going to be a great birthday!

B Listen again. How are they going to celebrate each event? Complete the chart.

12 Health talk

A Listen. What is a different way to say each sentence or question? Number these sentences or questions from 1 to 6.

1. How are you?
2. I feel awful.
3. What's the matter?
4. My stomach hurts.
5. Don't stay up late.
6. I have sore eyes.

B Listen again. Check the best response.

13 Where is it?

A Listen. Where do the people want to go? Number the pictures from 1 to 4.

1. WOMAN: Excuse me, where's the supermarket?
   MAN: Oh, um, it's on Center Street.
   WOMAN: Is it on the corner of First and Center?
   MAN: No. It's on Center Street, between the drugstore and the gas station.

2. WOMAN: Can you help me? I'm looking for the movie theater.
   MAN: Oh, sure. It's not far from here, on Main Street.
   WOMAN: Where on Main Street?
   MAN: Let's see . . . It's across from the department store.

3. MAN: Excuse me. Where's the bus stop?
   WOMAN: Um, it's on the corner of Center Avenue and First Street.
   MAN: Is it across from the drugstore?
   WOMAN: No, no, it's next to the hotel.
   MAN: Next to the hotel. Thanks a lot.

4. WOMAN: Excuse me. I think I'm lost. I need the post office.
   MAN: The post office? It's on the corner of Center Avenue and First Street. It's across from the drugstore.
   WOMAN: Thanks a lot!

B Listen again. Where are the places? Correct the mistakes.

14 Last weekend

A Listen to the conversations. Did Gary, Debra, and Brian have good weekends? Check Yes or No.

WOMAN: Hi, Gary. Did you have a good weekend?
GARY: Yeah, it was great. On Saturday, my friends and I played basketball. Then, in the evening, we watched a movie on television.
WOMAN: That sounds like fun. So what did you do on Sunday?
GARY: Oh, Sunday was my dad's birthday.
WOMAN: Great! Did you have a party?
GARY: Yeah. In the afternoon my mom and I cooked a lot of food. Then we had the party in the evening. We all had a great time.

MAN: Did you have a good weekend, Debra?
DEBRA: Well . . . not really. I did laundry on Saturday morning. Then I shopped for groceries on Saturday afternoon.
MAN: Did you go out Saturday night?
DEBRA: No. I didn't. I studied for a test. And I cleaned the house all day on Sunday.
MAN: Wow! You worked hard over the weekend.

WOMAN: Did you go anywhere this weekend, Brian?
BRIAN: Yes, I did. On Saturday, my girlfriend and I went to the beach.
WOMAN: Oh? Did you have a good time?
BRIAN: Oh, yeah! In the morning, we went swimming. Then we had a picnic on the beach.
WOMAN: Sounds nice.
BRIAN: Then we met some friends and played volleyball. We had a great game!

B Listen again. Put each person's activities in time order from 1 to 4.

15 Time line

A Listen to an interview with an actress. Write the years you hear on the time line.

INTERVIEWER: So, Lana, when were you born?
LANA: I was born in 1983.
INTERVIEWER: Were you born in the U.S.?
LANA: No, actually I was born in China.
INTERVIEWER: Interesting. Did you start acting in China?
LANA: No, I didn't. I started acting here, in the U.S.
INTERVIEWER: Tell me, when did you move here?
LANA: Let's see, I was 7 years old. So I moved here in 1990.
INTERVIEWER: And then when did you start acting?
LANA: In 1994.
INTERVIEWER: Wow, you were pretty young.
LANA: Yes, I was only 11. I actually got my first acting job just two years later. I was only 13.
INTERVIEWER: So you got your first acting job in 1996?
LANA: That's right.
INTERVIEWER: What did you do?
LANA: Oh, I did small roles for television on weekends. I did that until I graduated from high school – in 2001.
INTERVIEWER: And then what did you do?
LANA: Well, for two years I did more small roles for television. And then I got my first movie role in 2003.
INTERVIEWER: Was that exciting?
LANA: Oh, yes. It changed my life. . . .

B Listen again. Complete the sentences with the correct years.

16 Hi, Kate!

Listen. There are three mistakes in each message. Correct the mistakes.

1. [beep] Hi, Kate. This is Don. My sister is visiting me, and we're going to see a movie tonight. Do you want to come? Please call me by four o'clock today.

2. [beep] Hi, Kate. This is Bill. Sorry I missed your call. I was in the shower. I'd love to have dinner with you tomorrow, but I can't. I have to work late. Sorry!

3. [beep] Hi, Kate. This is Howard. I was in the hospital last week, so I missed our English class. What did we study? Please call me at home. The number is 555-4590. Thanks.

Self-study answer key

9
A Top row: 6, 2, 3, 7; Bottom row: 5, 1, 8, 4
B ~~cake~~   ~~hamburgers~~   ~~potato chips~~   ~~vegetables~~

10
A 2, 1, 4, 3
B 1. What sports do you watch?   3. When do you practice?
2. How often do you practice?   4. Where do you play?

11
A/B

Event	Date	What are they going to do?
John's graduation	June 15th	have a party
Amy and Jeff's wedding	June 22nd	give them a present
Parents' anniversary	July 10th	go out for dinner
Kenny's birthday	August 9th	have a picnic

12
A 1. How do you feel?
2. I don't feel well.
3. What's wrong?
4. I have a stomachache.
5. Go to bed early.
6. My eyes are sore.

B 1. I'm just fine, thanks.
2. Maybe I can help.
3. I have a cold.
4. Take some antacid.
5. That's good advice.
6. I'm sorry to hear that.

13
A 2, 3, 4, 1
B 1. ~~across from~~   between
2. ~~next to~~   across from
3. ~~across from~~   next to
4. ~~Fourth~~   First

14
A Gary: Yes   Debra: No   Brian: Yes
B Gary: 4, 3, 1, 2   Debra: 1, 2, 3, 4   Brian: 3, 4, 1, 2

15
A 1983, 1990, 1994, 1996, 2001, 2003
B 1. 1983   3. 1996   5. 1994
2. 2001   4. 1990   6. 2003

16
1. ~~brother~~   sister
~~tomorrow night~~   tonight
~~5:00~~   4:00
2. ~~yard~~   shower
~~lunch~~   dinner
~~study for a test~~   work late
3. ~~Mexico~~   the hospital
~~English~~   math
~~555-4509~~   555-4590

Appendix

Countries, nationalities, and languages

This is a partial list of countries, nationalities, and languages.

Countries	Nationalities	Countries	Nationalities	Countries	Nationalities
Argentina	Argentine	Haiti	Haitian	Peru	Peruvian
Australia	Australian	Honduras	Honduran	the Philippines	Filipino
Austria	Austrian	India	Indian	Poland	Polish
Bolivia	Bolivian	Indonesia	Indonesian	Portugal	Portuguese
Brazil	Brazilian	Ireland	Irish	Puerto Rico	Puerto Rican
Cambodia	Cambodian	Israel	Israeli	Russia	Russian
Canada	Canadian	Italy	Italian	Saudi Arabia	Saudi Arabian
Chile	Chilean	Japan	Japanese	Singapore	Singaporean
China	Chinese	Jordan	Jordanian	Somalia	Somalian
Colombia	Colombian	Korea	Korean	South Africa	South African
Costa Rica	Costa Rican	Laos	Laotian	Spain	Spanish
Cuba	Cuban	Lebanon	Lebanese	Sudan	Sudanese
the Dominican Republic	Dominican	Malaysia	Malaysian	Sweden	Swedish
Ecuador	Ecuadorian	Mexico	Mexican	Switzerland	Swiss
Egypt	Egyptian	Morocco	Moroccan	Tanzania	Tanzanian
El Salvador	El Salvadoran	Nepal	Nepalese	Thailand	Thai
England	English	the Netherlands	Dutch	Turkey	Turkish
France	French	New Zealand	New Zealander	the United Kingdom (the U.K.)	British
Germany	German	Nicaragua	Nicaraguan	the United States (the U.S.)	American
Ghana	Ghanian	Nigeria	Nigerian	Uruguay	Uruguayan
Greece	Greek	Panama	Panamanian	Venezuela	Venezuelan
Guatemala	Guatemalan	Paraguay	Paraguayan	Vietnam	Vietnamese

Languages

Afrikaans	English	Hebrew	Japanese	Portuguese	Swedish
Arabic	French	Hindi	Korean	Russian	Thai
Chinese	German	Indonesian	Malay	Spanish	Turkish
Dutch	Greek	Italian	Polish	Swahili	Vietnamese

Irregular verbs

Present	Past	Present	Past	Present	Past
(be) am/is, are	was, were	have	had	sing	sang
become	became	know	knew	sit	sat
buy	bought	leave	left	sleep	slept
come	came	make	made	speak	spoke
do	did	meet	met	swim	swam
drink	drank	pay	paid	take	took
drive	drove	read	read /rɛd/	teach	taught
eat	ate	ride	rode	think	thought
feel	felt	run	ran	wear	wore
get	got	say	said /sɛd/	write	wrote
give	gave	see	saw		
go	went	sell	sold		

Acknowledgments

Illustrations

Tim Foley 74 (*bottom*), 92 (*top*), SS10, SS13
Jeff Grunewald IA11, IA13
Randy Jones *v*, 61, 66, 67, 72, 74 (*top*), 79 (*bottom*), 80, 81, 95 (*top*), 100, 103, IA10
Wally Neibart 88

Ben Shannon 59, 75, 79 (*top*), 82, 87, 96, 102
Dan Vasconcellos 85, 94, 95 (*bottom*)
Sam Whitehead 64, 89, 92 (*bottom*), 99, 106, 108

Photo credits

59 (*apples*) © Photos.com; (*all others*) © Steven Ogilvy
60 (*left to right*) © Steven Ogilvy; © Steven Ogilvy; © George Kerrigan/Digital Eyes
61 © Patty Eckersley/Getty Images
62 © Jose Luis Pelaez/Corbis
63 (*mochi*) © George Kerrigan/Digital Eyes; (*all others*) © Steven Ogilvy
65 (*top*) © Getty Images; (*bottom*) © DiMaggio/Kalish/Corbis
66 © Amwell/Getty Images
69 (*clockwise from top left*) © AP/Wide World Photos; © Bob Martin/Getty Images; © Paul A. Souders/Corbis; © Paul H. Nilson/Imperial Valley Press/AP/Wide World Photos
71 (*left to right*) © Alamy; © age Fotostock; © Larry Williams/Corbis; © Getty Images
73 (*top row, left to right*) © Michael Keller/Index Stock Imagery; © Giantstep/Photonica; © Jim Cummins/Getty Images; © Alistair Berg/Getty Images; (*bottom row, left to right*) © Ariel Skelley/Corbis; © Jose Luis Pelaez/Corbis; © GDT/Getty Images; © Jason Dewey/Getty Images
76 (*left to right*) © Nik Wheeler/Corbis; © Peter Sanders/HAGA/AP/Wide World Photos; © Eriko Sugita/Reuters/Corbis
77 (*clockwise from top left*) © Roderick Chen/SuperStock; © Bill Walsh/SuperStock; © Harvey Lloyd/SuperStock; © Paul Barton/Corbis
78 © Steven Ogilvy
80 (*all photos*) © Steven Ogilvy
83 (*number 2*) © Sean Justice/Getty Images; (*number 3*) © Chris Rogers/Corbis; (*number 5*) © David Stoecklein/Corbis; (*number 6*)

© Michael A. Keller Studio/Corbis; (*number 7*) © Roy Morsch/Corbis; (*number 8*) © Michael A. Keller Studio/Corbis
86 (*top, left to right*) © David Young Wolff/Photo Edit; © Jose Luis Pelaez, Inc./Corbis; (*middle row, left to right*) © Peter Hvizdak/The Image Works; © SuperStock; © Elie Bernager/Getty Images; (*bottom row, left to right*) © Tony Freeman/Photo Edit; © Robert Brenner/Photo Edit; © Getty Images
89 (*top, left to right*) © Getty Images; © Danny Lehman/Corbis; © Corbis; (*bottom, left to right*) © Getty Images; © John Lamb/Getty Images; © Getty Images
91 (*clockwise from top left*) © Fred George/Getty Images; © Andreas Pollock/Getty Images; © Dan Lecca/Getty Images; © Thomas A. Kelly/Corbis
93 © Ellen B. Senisi/The Image Works
97 (*left to right*) © John Feingersh/Corbis; © Comstock; © Punchstock
99 © Carlos Alvarez/Getty Images
100 (*left to right*) © Bembaron Jeremy/Corbis Sygma; © Reuters/Corbis; © Eric Robert/Corbis Sygma; © Rufus F. Folkks/Corbis; © Sergio Moraes/Reuters/Corbis
101 © Paul Chesley/Getty Images
102 (*left to right*) © Rufus F. Folkks/Corbis; © Paul Sutton/Duomo/Corbis; © Gregory Pace/Corbis; © Jeff Vespa/WireImage
104 © Corbis
105 © Jim Ruymen/Reuters/Corbis
107 (*top*) © Alamy; (*bottom*) © Larry Williams/Corbis
108 (*top row, left to right*) © Chuck Savage/Corbis; © Tom & Dee Ann

McCarthy/Corbis; © Neal Preston/Corbis; (*bottom, left to right*) © David Butow/Corbis Saba; © Ron Watts/Corbis
109 © Lisa Peardon/Getty Images
110 © Mary Kate Denny/Photo Edit
111 (*top row, left to right*) © Hugh Sitton/Getty Images; courtesy of Parrot Jungle Island, FL/www.parrotjungle.com; © Stacey Green/Workbook Stock; (*bottom, left to right*) © AP/Wide World Photos; © Peter Titmuss/Alamy
112 (*left to right*) © Bettmann/Corbis; © Underwood & Underwood/Corbis; © SuperStock
113 © Corbis
IA9 (*all photos*) © Steven Ogilvy
IA12 (*clockwise from top left*) © Gabe Palmer/Corbis; © VCG/Getty Images; © Mark Scott/Getty Images; © Getty Images; © Syracuse Newspapers/The Image Works; © Alamy
IA14 (*left*) © Myrleen Ferguson Cate/Photo Edit; (*right, top to bottom*) © Don Smetzer/Getty Images; © Norbert Schäfer/Corbis; © Michael Newman/Photo Edit
IA15 (*top row, left to right*) Courtesy of Natsu Ifill; © Punchstock; © Ross Whitaker/Getty Images; © Jonathan Nourok/Photo Edit; (*bottom row, left to right*) © Tony Garcia/Getty Images; © Peter Beck/Corbis; © Mike Malyszko/Getty Images; courtesy of Natsu Ifill
SS9 (*top row, left to right*) © Alamy; © Photospin; © Corbis; © age Fotostock; (*bottom row*) (*vegetables*) © Corbis; (*all others*) © George Kerrigan/Digital Eyes